ROCK AND WATER

Dear Leslie,

Thanks so much.
Peace to you & yours !

ROCK
AND
WATER

THE POWER OF THOUGHT
THE PEACE OF LETTING GO

*Cognitive and Acceptance-Based Skills for
Greater Happiness in Everyday Living*

~~~

SCOTT COOPER

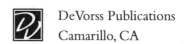

DeVorss Publications
Camarillo, CA

ROCK AND WATER
Copyright ©2017
by Scott Cooper

ISBN: 9780875168968
First Printing, 2017

DeVorss & Company, Publisher
P.O. Box 1389
Camarillo CA 93011-1389
www.devorss.com

Printed in the United States of America

Library of Congress Cataloging-in-Publication Data

Cooper, Scott, author.
Title: Rock and water : the power of thought and the peace of letting go :
     cognitive- and acceptance-based skills for greater happiness in everyday living
     / Scott Cooper.
Description: Camarillo, CA : DeVorss Publications, [2017] | Includes
     bibliographical references.
Identifiers: LCCN 2017016837 (print) | LCCN 2017036182 (ebook) |
     ISBN 9780875168975 (ebook) | ISBN 9780875168968 (pbk. : alk. paper)
Subjects: LCSH: Happiness. | Thought and thinking. | Social acceptance. |
     Cognitive psychology.
Classification: LCC BF575.H27 (ebook) | LCC BF575.H27 C667 2017 (print) |
     DDC 158.1—dc23
LC record available at https://lccn.loc.gov/2017016837

TABLE OF CONTENTS

TABLE OF CONTENTS

Part Two
Water—The Peace of Letting Go

To Adam, Jackson, and Brooke

ROCK AND WATER

We Were Meant to Be on This Planet

~~~

The pursuit of human happiness is built into the cosmos . . . really.

The highly specific laws of physics and the explosive birth of the universe provided everything necessary to produce life. The development of life on Earth hasn't been precisely predictable, but it hasn't been random either. It's clear that life on Earth occurs only down certain pathways and takes on only certain forms, and it does so quite abundantly.

We humans were meant to be in this world. Admittedly, it doesn't always feel this way. When I'm sitting in a traffic jam on the Golden Gate Bridge or sick in bed with the flu or catching a glimpse of certain reality TV shows, life does not feel supremely purposeful. And more painfully, when I read much of anything about the history of human warfare or see headlines of tragic accidents in my local newspaper, life can seem as if it were not meant for humans at all. As William S. Burroughs once wrote, "After one look at this planet, any visitor from outer space would say, 'I want to see the manager!' "

But once here, some things become pretty obvious. The clear

earthy purposes of our human body are survival and reproduction. We are born into bodies that over eons have developed natural faculties to help us function and survive in this world and allow us to provide the same for our offspring. But it's also clear that the purpose of an advanced human mind goes well beyond survival needs by allowing us to experience life and the universe in uniquely personal ways that, in turn, go well beyond physical survival. Our minds allow us to experience the following:

- Selfhood and personality
- Family, friends, and humanity
- A physical body and a natural world
- The ability to do and create
- Reasoning, imagination, and emotion
- Knowledge, science, and wonder
- Language, art, and music
- Beauty and wisdom
- Joy and suffering
- Good and evil
- Great uncertainty and the freedom and choice-making that come with it
- The challenge of working with and through an imperfect world

Believing that the sole purpose of a human mind is physical survival seems akin to believing that the sole purpose of a Boeing 747 is to blow leaves.

Among all our experiences, we humans are innately drawn to wanting to feel happiness—defined in scientific parlance as "subjective well-being" (or as "no worries" in my kids' jargon). Among all our possibilities, happiness is of compelling, fundamental, instinctive interest to each of us. We are driven to engage in those activities that we think will make our lives better (everything from getting a salary increase to spending a weekend in Disneyland) and avoiding what we think will make our lives worse (everything from putting on too much weight to spending a *week* in Disneyland).

Since ancient times, humankind has put a lot of time and energy into determining how to best obtain happiness (especially among the ancient Greek and Roman philosophers and among sages within the Jewish, Hindu, Taoist, Confucian, Buddhist, Christian, and Islamic traditions). For thinkers such as Socrates, Plato, and the Stoics, the most fundamental question was how people should best live. Their general conclusions were to have reverence for the universe, live justly, and accept what we cannot change.

In modern times, beyond the well-considered observations and reasoning of sages, we have the benefit of academic specialists who survey and study humans and strive to identify the factors that seem to accompany human well-being. According to Dr. Ed Diener, an international expert in the study of happiness from the University of Pennsylvania, research has found that the following five core factors can contribute to human happiness:

1. Loving relationships
2. Work satisfaction
3. Physical and mental health
4. Sufficient material well-being
5. Finding meaning (spirituality)

But these factors lead to subjective well-being only if they result in us having satisfying thoughts and feelings *inside*—and only if we develop the ability to cope *internally* with life experiences that don't go well. We can have good friends and a satisfying job and still be unhappy. We can have all the food, shelter, clothing, and lottery winnings imaginable and still worry. We can fully partic-ipate in faith communities or other supportive social groups and still have self-doubt and anxiety. On the other hand, we can expe-rience hardship and tragedy and still find inner peace and strength. We can live with less material wealth and still be content. We do not fully experience well-being until we experience it *internally*. As Aristotle wrote, "Happiness is an activity of the soul," an *internal* activity that requires some conscious effort.

Another academic expert on the study of happiness, Dr. Sonja Lyubomirsky of the University of California, Riverside, has found that the happiest people in her studies (1) spend a great amount of time with family and friends, (2) are often the first to lend a helping hand, (3) savor life's enjoyable activities, (4) engage in physical exer-cise, and (5) are deeply committed to lifelong goals and ambitions.

But again, for the happiest people, these more external behav-iors are accompanied by having satisfying and helpful thoughts and feelings *inside*. Such people are given to expressing gratitude, perceiving life with general optimism, and learning to internally cope with life's challenges. Additionally, Dr. Lyubomirsky and her colleagues believe, based on their own and others' studies, that approximately 50 percent of our happiness is based on our own individual natural genetic-happiness set point (or, how happy we are hardwired to be), 40 percent on our selected thinking and behaviors, and only 10 percent on our life circumstances, such as material wealth. Their research suggests that there is room (at least 50 percent worth) for each of us to make a difference when it comes to our personal well-being.

It should be noted that enhancing our inner well-being is not only good for our mental life, it's good for our bodies. In tracing the lives of children into adulthood over a thirty-year period, researchers at Harvard University found that optimism can cut the risk of coro-nary heart disease by half. The protective effects of hopefulness and emotional balance are physiologically distinct and measureable.

Prologue

Long-term unhappiness and stress can add wear and tear to our biological systems in ways that eventually lead to serious illness. *Rock and Water* was written to provide access to basic skills for enhancing our happiness. These skills are based primarily on modern research and practice in the fields of cognitive psychology and mindfulness/acceptance practice. Cognitive psychology is grounded in the theory that our happiness is strongly influenced by our thinking. It's not so much a situation that brings unhappiness, but rather our *perception* of a situation. If we think something is bad—whether it's truly bad or not—we will likely feel bad inside. By consciously modifying our thinking, we can perceive events more reasonably and feel better emotionally. More than 500 outcome studies since the 1970s have demonstrated the efficacy of cognitive-behavioral therapy in dealing with a wide range of issues relating to mental well-being (as outlined in *Clinical Psychological Review* 26, pages 17–31, 2006).

Mindfulness is grounded in the practice of using our conscious awareness to pay attention to things in the present moment in a nonjudgmental, nonreactive way. Formal mindfulness in the form of meditation has been practiced in the East for millennia, often in the Buddhist tradition (but also in the Hindu and Christian traditions) in which conscious awareness has a specific point of focus (often the breath or a unique word, or mantra). Acceptance is a modern approach to mental health that incorporates mindfulness and other techniques to help people accept rather than avoid unpleasant mental events that are not easy to change, enabling people to live their lives more fully in the midst of life's difficulties. The effect of both mindfulness and acceptance can be to inspire a more relaxed, nonjudgmental approach to life (as opposed to the emotional turmoil that can come from ongoing mental judgment and strife). Research over the past few decades confirms that mindfulness practice can reduce stress and anxiety (a review of such research is found in *Psychotherapy* 48 (2), pages 198–208,

2011). Similarly, acceptance has demonstrated clinical success in helping people deal more effectively with anxiety-related difficulties (as discussed in *Behavior Therapy* 35, pages 35–54, 2004).

It is certainly the case that modern medicine can play an important role in alleviating emotional pain. But medicine alone can't change the thoughts and behaviors that contribute to unhappiness. What the findings and real-life experience coming out of cognitive- and acceptance-based approaches to emotional health teach us is that we can enhance our well-being by doing the following:

- Modifying habits of thinking and behavior
- Adopting sensible core beliefs
- Accepting—rather than mentally battling—things that don't matter or that we can't change (including difficult thoughts and emotions)

I've been a student of philosophy and science for much of my adult life. I've also been actively engaged in efforts as a youth advocate to convey tools of well-being to young people and have written a few books on social-coping skills for children. This latter involvement led me to study and pull together research-based verbal, behavioral, and cognitive tools to help young people and their parents deal with the sometimes difficult social worlds that young people have to navigate (which in turn led to the books *Sticks and Stones* and *Speak Up and Get Along!*). I've become convinced that there are practical, common-sense skills coming out of contemporary work in cognitive-behavioral psychology and out of a broader mainstream focus on mindfulness/acceptance practice that can contribute to the happiness of all of us—tools that add much practical substance to core principles of human happiness that have been considered and taught through the ages. The purpose of this book, as with my previous books, is to provide these tools in a clear and usable form.

Often, cognitive-behavioral psychology and mindfulness/ acceptance practice are treated separately and in isolation. This book presents these concepts in a complementary form, applying two simple metaphors from nature: *rock*, which symbolizes the strong personal platform that reasonable thinking and sensible beliefs can provide for our lives, and *water*, which symbolizes the peace that can come to our lives by learning to let go of things we can't easily change or that don't matter.

You may use this book in any way you choose. You can work through Parts One and Two and each skill in sequence or skip around to the skills that seem most relevant. At the end of each skill, you'll find a summary for easy reference. *Rock and Water* is not intended to be yet another list of things to do and to be. It's meant to be a buffet of practical ideas—some of which may have relevance and value for your life.

I'm an outdoors person and throughout my life I've been powerfully inspired (and sometimes quite mesmerized) by the soothing peace to be found in nature's pleasing interplay between rock and water. Whether by way of a trickling mountain brook in the Mayacamas Mountains, the thunderous, frothy beaches of the Mendocino coastline, or a fresh, pristine lake found in a granite basin in the High Sierras—the sight, sound, and feel of rock and water have brought me much joy and refreshment. Not to mention that there is nothing quite as invigorating as diving from a granite boulder into a cold mountain river on a hot summer day! It's with good, personal reason that my only daughter is named Brooke.

Just as rock and water wander together seamlessly throughout the natural world, the hope for this book is that it will provide you with an integrated resource for greater happiness to help with the meandering and unpredictable ups and downs of your own life.

*I gave heed to the confiding stream,
mingled freely with the flowers and light,
and shared in the confidence of their
exceeding peace.*

JOHN MUIR

Part One

ROCK

THE POWER OF THOUGHT

Upgrade Your Mood by Upgrading Your Thinking

~~~

You may not control all the events that happen to you, but you can decide not to be reduced by them.

MAYA ANGELOU

I remember quite well the day I flunked a critical finance course when I was in graduate school. I was married and without much income and really needed to graduate and get a job. If I failed this course it would require that I take another semester of college, which I just couldn't afford to do. I felt depressed, so as soon as I could, I went into the woods—my place of solace—and found a beautiful, active stream to sit by. The flow and sound of water and the beauty and smell of the moss-tinged fir and redwood trees changed my attitude. I gradually gained perspective and felt better. Somehow by the end of the semester I ended up doing fine in the class, and my initial feeling of despair turned into extreme relief. In retrospect, from a lifetime's perspective, this episode was a minor bump in the road among all the things that can happen to a human being. But at the time it *felt* very big.

Feelings are dynamic. Without our emotions we wouldn't know the wonder of true love, the awe of a desert sunset, the fun of a summertime softball game, or the pleasure of a good book. We wouldn't know the satisfaction we feel when we finish washing the dishes—or the peace we can feel sitting in the forest. Joy, love, fun, enthusiasm, surprise, peace, and wonder are the emotional blessings of our lives. The poet E. E. Cummings captured the spirit of these positive feelings when he wrote:

"I thank you God for this most amazing day,

for the leaping greenly spirits of trees, and

for the blue dream of sky and for everything

which is natural, which is infinite, which is yes. "

But of course, as we all know too well, our natural feelings don't just bring us joy and satisfaction and say yes. They can be grouchy, unpleasant, and painful and shout out no. These unpleasant emotions can be quite important. Fear can help us flee from danger. Worry can help us prepare for the future. Anger can help us stop others from doing harm. Guilt can stop us from doing harm ourselves. Sorrow can help us heal when we've experienced a traumatic event. Physical and emotional pain, as much as we don't like either one of them, have a purpose.

Scientists tell us that our unpleasant emotions are mostly survival emotions—an impulse to action driven by the amygdala, an almond-shaped cluster of interconnected structures sitting atop the human brainstem. The amygdala quickly alerts our whole body when we perceive something as threatening or distasteful. It triggers hormonal secretions into our bloodstream that prepare the body for fight and flight. The neocortex, on the other hand, processes the information more slowly, allowing people to evaluate an event with thought rather than emotion.

This is why we jump out of our shoes when a friend dangles a rubber snake in front of us, settle down once we realize the snake is not real, and begin to consider how we will make our friend pay in some form.

Scientists also tell us that these survival emotions provide us with a built-in "negativity bias," meaning that we're more strongly influenced by our negative emotions than our positive ones (a point that politicians continue to take advantage of in their advertising). This may be why marriage researcher John Gottman has found that heathy marriages generally require about five positive communications to offset each negative communication, and the research of Marcial Losada and Emily Heaphy suggests that higher effectiveness in the workplace requires about six praises to counterbalance one blunt criticism. Because of this natural negativity bias, we may experience unpleasant emotions too intensely or too often, even when we don't need them. When unpleasant emotions are not needed, they end up being unproductive emotional noise that does us no good. Zen teachers sometimes compare this emotional noise to a very active "monkey" jumping around in our heads. These monkeys can be real troublemakers, shaking us up and wearing us down. But we're also born with the ability to calm down these monkeys through the power of our thoughts.

We experience the strong connection between thoughts and feelings on a daily basis. If I think a friend has called me a "hack" (a thought), I may feel insulted (a feeling). If I find out it was a bad rumor (a thought), I feel fine again (a feeling). If I think that I messed up on a sales call at work (a thought), I might feel discouraged (a feeling). If I remind myself that "this is just part of life," "nobody's perfect," or "you win some, you lose some" (thoughts), I feel better (a feeling). Or, as in my college experience, if I think I've blown a class and feel crappy, I feel better once I gain perspective or end up actually passing the class.

And so it goes in matters large and small. Here are a few more examples:

- If we think a situation is hopeless, we will likely feel hopeless. If we think patient thoughts, we will feel more patient.
- If we think that a person poses a real threat, we will feel fear or anger. If we think kind thoughts about someone, we will feel affection toward that person.
- If we think our lives are not worthwhile, we will feel less worthwhile. If we think our lives are generally good, life will feel more satisfying, and our subjective well-being will be enhanced.

My wonderful, emotionally honest mother used to sometimes tell me on a stormy winter day in our small Northern California town that rainy days could make her feel a little "blue." But it wasn't literally the drops of water that made my mother feel this way. On the other hand, her sunshiny rancher father in Idaho could be standing in a flooded basement and with a big smile on his face announce that he "sprang a leak!" Not everyone feels blue on a rainy day and not everyone can look upon a flooded basement with good humor. We each perceive things differently. The thoughts and perceptions swirling around in our minds are what prompt each of us to respond to events so differently. But we do have the ability to change our perceptions.

Sometimes our thoughts and perceptions solidify into beliefs. Beliefs are like rock. They are perceptions that have become concrete assumptions. But sometimes beliefs are seriously mistaken. For millennia, people believed that the Earth was flat (and they wouldn't dare sail their ships out too far) and that earthquakes, volcanic explosions, and other catastrophes were caused by their gods (and they weren't above sacrificing their friends and family members to make those gods happy). These were core assumptions that were taken for granted, and they were completely false. They also had a seriously negative impact on how people behaved. Likewise, our beliefs about ourselves, others, and the world become accepted conclusions over time. They become assumptions that we don't think much about once they've become beliefs.

Beliefs are quite important because we live our lives based on them. Cognitive scientists tell us that core beliefs lead to rules for living, which in turn lead to automatic thoughts, emotional responses, and behaviors. For example, if I adopt a strong, core belief that life should be easy and fun, I'll carry around an unwritten rule that the "hard stuff" should be avoided. This rule in turn will crank up the "It's too hard, I can't do it" kind of thinking that will keep me from carrying out important activities. Ironically, I may avoid the challenges, work, events, and relationships that would have made my life more fun and in the end, easier. All for the want of a more realistic, sturdy belief such as "Life isn't always fun and easy; it requires effort and I can do hard stuff when I need to." If I adopt the core belief that I'm less worthwhile if people disapprove of me, I'll likely feel anxious inside if I think somebody doesn't like me. I may end up spending too much time and energy considering people's opinions of me and trying to please them. And this may all come at the cost of my own legitimate needs and self-interest. Again, all for want of a more realistic belief such as "I'm a regular human being with strengths and weaknesses; it's good to be kind, but I don't need to be liked."

As an outdoors person who enjoys birding on occasion, a fun scene for me is watching a mother duck in the water with her ducklings faithfully paddling right behind her moving quickly with each twist and turn of the mother. Cognitive specialists tell us that this happens with our mental lives. Our beliefs and thoughts lead the way, and our emotions faithfully follow right behind. The specialists sometimes diagram the relationship between beliefs, rules, thoughts, and emotions in the manner below.

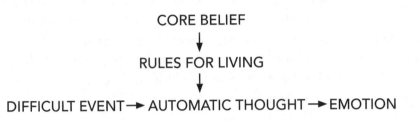

If we experience a difficult event, automatic thoughts and emotions, which are fundamentally driven by our beliefs and rules for living, often cascade. Whenever a difficult event happens, our core beliefs and rules for living will be there to generate the thoughts that will either keep us going or pull us down. If our beliefs and thinking habits bring us down, we need to get better ones.

Betty Ford, the former American First Lady, grew up comfortably in Grand Rapids, Michigan. Her happy family life was painfully interrupted by the death of her father when she was just sixteen. She was a talented dancer and eventually studied under the legendary choreographer and dancer Martha Graham. After weathering a difficult first marriage, she eventually married a young attorney—Gerald Ford. She successfully raised a family of four children and became a popular First Lady.

However, as chronicled in her book *Betty: A Glad Awakening*, despite all her successes she also carried burdensome beliefs about personal inadequacy and perfectionism. These beliefs led to emotional pain, which along with physical ailments, contributed to her becoming severely addicted to alcohol and pain medication in midlife. Her core beliefs of inadequacy led to thoughts of worthlessness, which led to depression, which led to alcoholism (aside from any genetic tendency she may have had). Her drinking problem only led to a greater sense of inadequacy and thus to a painful downward spiral. But with the help of her family, Betty Ford made the choice at the age of sixty to get help and transform her life. She worked through the thinking, beliefs, and behaviors that were contributing to both her emotional pain and her addictions. Not only did she change her own life but she urged and inspired others to do the same. She once wrote, "You never know what you can do until you have to do it." Today the Betty Ford Center continues to help scores of people transform their lives.

We experience both pleasant and unpleasant events every day. Sometimes we experience serious events that are extremely difficult to cope with: the death of a loved one, illness, or serious financial setbacks. But our thinking can make even everyday events much worse than they really are. Our thoughts are very powerful. They can make us feel better or worse, stronger or weaker, hopeful or hopeless. If our thoughts are exaggerated and overly negative, we are likely to experience unhappy emotions when we don't need or want them. This in turn can affect our behavior and decision-making. As with Betty Ford, our thinking can contribute to both despair and recovery—to both pain and gain.

There are many simple ways to experiment with and experience the direct connection between thoughts and feelings for ourselves. Here are a few examples:

- Think of one of your happiest childhood memories in detail. How does it make you feel? Think of one of your saddest childhood memories. How does that make you feel? Even though these are not current events, just the thought of them affects how we feel.

- Imagine in detail the most pleasant, enjoyable place you've been to. How does that perception make you feel? It's difficult to have unpleasant feelings while thinking about a very peaceful and enjoyable place or experience. Jill Bolte Taylor, the Harvard-based neuroanatomist who wrote *My Stroke of Insight*, uses the approach of simply thinking about a person or activity that brings her pleasure as her form of meditation whenever she feels overly stressed.

- Think about a special loved one with acceptance, kindness, and understanding (letting go for a moment of his or her flaws and weaknesses). How does it make you feel toward him or her in that moment? Thoughts of kindness can lead to feelings of kindness.

- Think about a few things you're grateful for. How does that make you feel? A study published by Emmons and McCullough in 2003 suggests that simply writing down and reflecting on what we're grateful and thankful for on a weekly basis can enhance our emotional attitude.

- Since thoughts affect feelings, what we bring into our minds by way of what we read, see, hear, and listen to can also affect how we feel. Notice how you feel when you read or watch something inspiring or visit with a good friend who lifts you up as opposed to how you feel when you read bad news in the newspaper or hang out with overly negative people.

It may seem simplistic, but it is really true that one of the key portals to well-being is to have reasonable thoughts and beliefs. And thus one of the critical skills we need to enhance well-being is to upgrade our thinking if it is churning up unpleasant emotions.

SUMMARY FOR SKILL 1

Upgrade Your Mood by Upgrading Your Thinking

A good place to start with unnecessary, unpleasant emotions is to change up our thinking.

We will feel more hopeful if we consciously think hopeful thoughts.

We will feel more kindness toward others—friends, families, and even strangers—if we think about them with kindness.

We will feel less anxious about problems if we gain perspective and think of solutions.

We will feel better about the world if we consider the good as well as the bad.

Filling our minds with too much of what we don't enjoy or those things that bring us worries will do little good for our well-being.

Some of this is influenced by our natural temperament, but perhaps fifty percent of it can also be affected by the thoughts and behaviors we select.

We can enhance the type of people, activities, media (Internet, publications, TV, movies), and conscious thoughts, images, and memories that we bring into our mental lives to enhance and uplift our feelings.

Noticing and Responding to Thinking Mistakes

~~~

It is not the things themselves that disturb people,
but their judgment about those things.

EPICTETUS

Teddy Roosevelt had every reason to grow up with a bad attitude. He was unusually sickly and asthmatic as a child and struggled with health issues throughout much of his adult life. His father, the rock of his early life, died when Teddy was a young man, and his first wife died after only a few years of marriage (his wife and his mother both died on Valentine's Day 1884). He suffered early political defeats and experienced bouts of self-doubt. His beloved youngest son, Quentin, was killed in World War I. But Teddy is not remembered for the obstacles he faced or for his illnesses and trag-edies; he's remembered for his gusto for living. He's remembered for his optimistic outlook and for his fully engaged life—exploring the world, constantly learning, parenting actively, and engaging in robust physical activity and public service. His habits of thinking and action overcame the great difficulties of his circumstances. He once wrote, "I have never in my life envied a human being who lived an easy life; I have envied a great many people who led difficult lives and led them well."

This is not to say that Teddy Roosevelt did not have moments filled with deep despair and anxiety. He went into extended grieving and depression upon the death of his first wife and spent months in solitude in the Dakotas. On the day of his wife's death he wrote in his diary, "the light has gone out of my life." Like Roosevelt, we all experience a natural tapestry of pleasant and unpleasant emotions that come with our human condition. But if we experience the dark aspect of that "tapestry" too often, we can apply the power of thought to help strengthen our ability to cope. But how do we do this?

In the 1950s, scientists and psychologists began to look much more closely at the mental processes of thinking, perception, language, memory, attention, and problem-solving and eventually a new area of study called "cognitive psychology" emerged. Under this influence, in the 1960s new practical approaches and tools were developed to help people deal with anxiety and other unpleasant emotions. Much of the early development of cognitive therapy tools was pioneered by Dr. Aaron Beck at the University of Pennsylvania, a college of psychology that has produced experts in recent times who have become known for their emphasis on practical psychology. The initial framework of cognitive therapy was based on some simple ideas:

- If you chronically have unhappy feelings, thinking habits are likely part of the problem.
- You can train yourself to modify your thinking.
- As your thinking becomes more reasonable and less negative, your well-being increases.

Beck identified specific "cognitive distortions" that can contribute to unhappiness. Cognitive distortions, or "thinking mistakes," are stark, incomplete perceptions of life's events. These thinking mistakes are generally based on seeing things only one way without considering other factors. They are also commonly based on simplistically judging people and events rather than just factually describing them without judgment. If these thinking distortions develop into habits, they can result in chronic mental patterns that influence our feelings and behavior.

At its core, cognitive therapy is about becoming more reasonable and flexible in how we think about ourselves, others, and the world. And this requires that we identify and respond to distortions in our thinking. In more recent times, a more comprehensive cognitive-behavioral therapy model has evolved, with the practical recognition that both thinking *and* behavior can influence emotions (see the Skill 8 chapter).

Dr. Beck and his protégés developed full descriptive lists of cognitive distortions to help professionals and lay people clearly identify such distortions in order to learn to respond to them (an excellent resource for further discussion on cognitive distortions is the popular trade book *Feeling Good* by David Burns, one of Beck's students). Modern lists of cognitive distortions can include up to fifteen categories. Below is a list of five common thinking mistakes and examples of rational responses. An important skill in enhancing emotional well-being is to become more aware of such errors and remind ourselves of why they're faulty.

1. **Exaggerating**—The perception that something is much worse than it really is, and it is often accompanied by words such as *always, completely,* and *never.* My wife has pointed out that sometimes I give into this thinking distortion, but I'm confident that I *never, ever* exaggerate. However I'm also confident that exaggeration can magically take relatively minor problems or flaws and turn them into unnecessarily big issues.

EXAGGERATING

IRRATIONAL RESPONSE	RATIONAL RESPONSE
"It was too hot today, so it was a horrible day."	"I'm completely exaggerating. Heat is a part of nature. I'm just in a bad mood."
"I broke up with my girlfriend, so I'll never have a girlfriend again."	"This is really exaggerated. It's very likely that I'll have another girlfriend someday."
"I didn't get a college degree, so I'm a loser."	"This is truly crazy thinking. Many people have not graduated from college. Are Abraham Lincoln, Steve Jobs, and Mother Teresa all losers? Really?"

2. **Seeing (or Forecasting) Only the Bad**—This one-sided, stark, incomplete thinking habit focuses only on one side--the bad side. Such thinking can taint our feelings about the past and present as well as our forecast for future events (by assuming the future will also be bad). Very few things in life are completely bad. This all-or-nothing thinking is faulty because it doesn't take enough other facts into consideration.

SEEING ONLY THE BAD

IRRATIONAL RESPONSE	RATIONAL RESPONSE
"The stock market crashed, so my life is over."	"I'm seeing just the dark side right now. I'm alive, and I have food and shelter. This is just one day in the stock market; other parts of my life today are just fine."
"My wife is completely inconsiderate, so I need a divorce."	"I'm exaggerating and only seeing one aspect of my wife. I need to remember all the good, the love we share, how much I value her, and try to first work through our problems."
"The world is getting worse all the time."	"I'm focusing on all the bad news events I read and hear about; there is plenty of good stuff happening, too. In many ways and for millions of people, the world is much better than it was a hundred years ago."
"Work will be boring today."	"Maybe, maybe not. But I'm sure to make it more that way by thinking this. What can I do today or this evening that would be really enjoyable?"

3. Labeling—By simply equating ourselves, others, or the world to one bad quality, we are applying a harsh mix of exaggeration and seeing only the bad. Instead of factually describing something ("It is what it is"), we apply a judgmental label ("It's bad!").

Labeling is illogically naming ourselves a "failure," rather than simply saying that we made a mistake. It's calling our coworker "lazy," instead of simply describing how he needs to work harder on the project. If we have become chronically cruel or abusive, then yes we deserve a bad label. But it's silly, illogical, and very detrimental to imply that we or others are not worthwhile simply because we're overweight, klutzy, or have the usual imperfections of a human being.

LABELING

IRRATIONAL RESPONSE	RATIONAL RESPONSE
"I'm not very good-looking."	"So what's the problem? I'm no movie star, but how many people are? If I'm implying that I'm not worthwhile because I'm not a "10," that's craziness. I would be not worthwhile if I were a psycho killer."
"He's from another country, so he's probably dangerous."	"I really don't know him or have any idea about who he is."
"I'm not good at fixing things, so I'm incompetent."	"Actually this isn't true. I'm not so great at fixing stuff around the house, but I'm pretty good at a lot of other things. Truth is, I don't put much time into trying to get good at fixing things."

4. **Extreme Blaming**—I'm well versed in applying unwarranted blame on occasion, and my wife might say that I would likely blame her for that. One of the curses of motherhood seems to be that whenever anything is lost or misplaced, mothers become the victims of 100 percent blame, stemming from family members large and small and their faulty-thinking habits. When we blame mothers, ourselves, or others out of proportion, we're assigning blame without reasonably considering all factors. Typically, extreme blaming is allocating 100 percent of the blame to one scapegoat (sometimes ourselves), with the irrational condemnation that comes with it. Even if it is 100 percent our fault, aren't we allowed to our human mistakes?

EXTREME BLAMING

IRRATIONAL RESPONSE	RATIONAL RESPONSE
"We lost the customer and it was all my coworker's fault."	"My coworker made a mistake, but even though we apologized, the customer still left. If the customer is going to be that unreasonable, then it's just as well we lost him."
"My friend won't talk to me anymore, and it's all because of me."	"It's too bad this happened, but it's part of life. Neither of us is perfect, and we both probably could have handled it better. But if she's a true friend, she'll talk to me in the future. If not, she won't."
"I stuttered during my speech, so I'm a complete screwup."	"My overall speech was not perfect, but it was just fine. Would I think that of someone else? I'm a regular person with strengths and weaknesses, not a screwup—whether I stutter or not."

5. **Emotional Reasoning**—Thinking that something is good (or bad) simply because we feel it's good (or bad), regardless of any evidence to the contrary, distorts our judgement and hampers our ability to see the factual reality. We overidentify with emotional sensations as critically important, as who we are or as truth even though sometimes emotional sensation is simply imperfect emotional "noise" passing through our minds.

Sometimes how we feel about things points us in the right direction (and it's important to initially hear out our hunches), but sometimes our feelings can be off target. And thoughts can be the same. Sometimes thoughts are helpful and true, and sometimes they are unhelpful and false, just aimless ruminations passing through.

EMOTIONAL REASONING

IRRATIONAL RESPONSE	RATIONAL RESPONSE
"I feel that guy is deceptive, so he must be deceptive."	"Holy cow! Impressions can be completely wrong. Just because I feel something doesn't make it so. I need to get some hard evidence."
"I feel lazy, therefore I am lazy."	"Jeez, I'm just feeling lazy. I'm not my feelings. I get stuff done once I get started."
"I feel hopeless, therefore I am hopeless."	"There's no doubt I'm feeling down, but feeling hopeless doesn't make me hopeless. It's just a feeling. I've got to pick myself back up and get going again."
"That guy said I'm selfish, so I must be."	"Thoughts are thoughts. I'm not perfect, but that guy's unreasonable thinking doesn't magically create reality."
"I had a bad thought, therefore I'm a bad person."	"Seriously? Thoughts are thoughts. Humans have all sorts of thoughts and emotions flow through them. Bad people do seriously harmful and dangerous things. I'm not perfect, but I'm also not any single thought that flows through my mind."

Sometimes when we feel anxious or worried, the flaws in our thinking are so immediately obvious when we stop and notice them that a quick intuitive rebuttal will do. Other times, it might be helpful to reflect a little more on the things we're telling ourselves. We can simply ask ourselves a few questions:

- What thought is making me feel this way?
- Am I exaggerating, seeing only the bad, labeling, or making some other thinking mistake?
- What does the evidence or logic tell me in this situation?
- What would I tell a best friend who came to me with this kind of thinking?
- What's the worst that would happen if this thought were true?
- If this thought is based on a problem I need to solve, what can I do to begin to solve it?
- If this thought is based on something I can't change, how long do I need to live with the thought? How useful is it to me?

J. K. Rowling, the author of the Harry Potter series, went through serious depression in her midtwenties. She had recently split up with her husband and was experiencing serious self-doubt, which led to further exaggerated thinking, which in turn led to her questioning her own core worth. She was ultimately able to revive herself, in part with the help of specialists in cognitive psychology, by working with her thinking and beliefs. Picking herself back up mentally enabled her to continue on her determined journey to literary and personal success. Of her experience, Rowling once said in an interview, "I have never been remotely ashamed of having been depressed. Never. What's to be ashamed of? I went through a really rough time, and I am quite proud that I got out of that."

Ancient Greek and Roman Stoic philosophers were clued in to this problem of distorted perceptions, or errors in judgment, and their influence on negative emotions. They were an active, popular influence in Greek and Roman societies between 350 BC and AD 200, and one of their key teachings was that it's not so much the situations themselves that bring us anxiety but our perception of those situations. But the Stoics never took their thinking one step further to discuss the *how* of changing those perceptions. They would have been heartened by the practical, reason-based ideas of modern cognitive-behavioral specialists in identifying and responding to thinking mistakes.

The former Roman slave and Stoic philosopher Epictetus, who lived between 55 and 135, stated, "And because of lack of practice, we are always piling up worries and fancying ... things to be graver than they really are." And the Roman Stoic philosopher/emperor of Rome, Marcus Aurelius, who lived between 121–180, wrote in his *Meditations*, "but those who do not observe the movements of their own minds must of necessity be unhappy."

What was true then remains true today: Our thoughts can make things worse. By noticing troublesome unpleasant feelings and the perceptions that accompany them, we can then begin to watch out for thinking mistakes and remind ourselves of why they're mistaken.

For those of us who have ongoing issues with worry, fear, and anxiety, cognitive specialists suggest keeping a "crib sheet" of common worrisome thoughts that come to us in our everyday lives, along with reasonable responses to them. We can then refer to these crib sheets in order to gradually learn to respond to counterproductive thinking. Keep a pad and pen handy if this works for you and jot down your own thinking mistakes and the best responses to counter them. (The boxes on the previous pages featuring five common thinking problems and their rational responses are a version of such a tool.)

Changing our thinking is not the whole story, of course. And sometimes, especially if we experience very difficult life events, it can feel like not nearly enough. In addition, feelings can be heavily influenced by our natural temperament and physiological makeup. But in dealing with the ups and downs of everyday living, working with distorted habits of thinking is clearly a helpful tool for enhancing our general well-being.

SUMMARY FOR SKILL 2

Noticing and Responding to Thinking Mistakes

Cognitive-behavioral experts maintain that an important skill that can benefit our well-being is the ability to notice and respond to common thinking mistakes that can make us feel more anxious and worried than we need to.

It helps to first understand what thinking mistakes (or cognitive distortions) are. Some of them are described in this chapter.

Applying this skill requires asking ourselves a few basic questions to uncover our thinking mistakes, and then determining which simple questions work best for us.

Review the questions on page 22 and consider keeping a crib sheet of your own common thinking mistakes and reasonable responses.

SKILL 3

Reasonable Optimism

~~~

The greatest weapon against stress is our ability
to choose one thought over another.

WILLIAM JAMES

If I had to guess, I would say that I'm by nature mildly pessimistic. I feel this to be true because I can relate so directly to the following quote from Robyn Ayers, "The good thing about being a pessimist is that I'm either always right or pleasantly surprised." And I do indeed feel pleasantly surprised when our Oakland Athletics win tight games or when I find a parking spot in San Francisco. My natural explanatory style tends toward assuming that things may not go well.

Each of us over time develops an explanatory style to help us explain life's events. And this style can make a big difference in terms of our resilience and well-being. If we see a dangerous storm brewing we can tell ourselves "no worries" or "we're doomed" or "let's get prepared, and hopefully we'll be okay." Unreasonable optimism sees only the sunshine and keeps us from being careful and prepared. Pessimism can immobilize us and make bad things worse by focusing only on the clouds. Reasonable optimism sees the clouds for what they are and takes action with hope for the future. Reasonable optimism has become my target explanatory style over time.

Dr. Martin Seligman, a specialist in the study of optimism from the University of Pennsylvania, contended in his book *Learned Optimism* that optimism isn't so much the power of positive thinking as it is the power of nonnegative thinking. Reasonable optimism is not so much wearing rose-tinted glasses as it is taking off overly dark lenses. We don't need to stand in front of a mirror and say "I'm wonderful." We just need to make sure to talk back to thoughts that say "I'm not worthwhile" or "life is terrible." A pessimistic explanatory style explains setbacks and difficulty as follows:

- Permanent ("It's going to last forever")
- Pervasive ("It's going to ruin everything")
- Personal ("It's all my fault")

An optimistic explanatory style explains setbacks as follows:

- Temporary ("This will pass")
- Isolated ("This is part of life")
- Not overly personal ("Everyone makes mistakes")

In Dr. Seligman's research on professional athletes, he found that the most successful athletes and sports teams tend to be the ones that have the most optimistic explanatory styles when things don't go well. Studies of professional baseball and basketball teams show a correlation between optimism (above and beyond how good a team is) and success in the game. All other components being equal, teams with players who explain losses with, "It wasn't our day" or "The other team just played well," outperform teams with players who explain such events with, "We just can't hit" or "We don't play with confidence." The bottom line is that we do ourselves no favors beating ourselves up when things don't go well. We're much better off if we can use our words to pick ourselves back up. As the ever-sunny Muhammad Ali put it, "I should be a postage stamp. That's the only way I'll ever get licked."

If a negative explanatory style becomes a habit, it can darken our lives and increase our sense of hopelessness and helplessness. Like any other thinking mistake, unreasonable pessimism is usually harsh and inflexible. It sees only the bad. The skill of reasonable optimism involves coming up with words and phrases for ourselves that trigger a more flexible perspective to help deal with setbacks. These phrases are likely different for each person. It's clear that for Ali, any phrase with the word *great* worked. As he put it, tongue in cheek, "My only fault is that I don't realize how great I really am." We each have words that can help us in response to overly pessimistic thinking. We can practice with such phrasing until we find words that resonate. A few possibilities are listed on page 30.

Viktor Frankl was born in Vienna to Jewish civil servants. He studied at the University of Vienna and became a neurologist and psychiatrist. After living under Nazi occupation in Austria, he and his wife were sent to the Auschwitz concentration camp, where they were separated. The only thing that kept him going was keeping the image of his wife in his mind and focusing on his love for her. He wrote:

"I understood how a man who has nothing left in this world may still know bliss, be it only for a brief moment, in the contemplation of his beloved. In a position of utter desolation, when a man cannot express himself in positive action, when his only achievement may consist in enduring his sufferings in the right way—an honorable way—in such a position man can, through loving contemplation of the image he carries of his beloved, achieve fulfillment."

REASONABLE OPTIMISM

PESSIMISTIC EXPLANATORY PHRASE	OPTIMISTIC COUNTER PHRASES
"It's going to ruin everything."	"It's not literally going to ruin everything." "What's the worst thing that can happen?" "It's a small part of life." "Is there something I can do to make it better?"
"It's all my fault."	"There were a lot of factors involved." "This is part of life." "Everyone makes mistakes." "I'll make up for it."
"This is terrible; it's way too hard."	"I just need to get started." "It won't kill me." "I can get through it." "I'll take it one little step at a time." "I'll get help if I need to."

Eventually Frankl's wife, mother, and brother all died in concentration camps. His only surviving family member was his sister. Despite experiencing overwhelming despair during the Holocaust, Frankl lived on to become a champion of finding hope, perspective, and meaning in life. He returned to a life of psychology and teaching, and he expressed his ideas in thirty-two books. He once wrote:

"We who lived in concentration camps can remember the men who walked through the huts comforting others, giving away their last piece of bread. They may have been few in number, but they offer sufficient proof that everything can be taken from a man but one thing: the last of the human freedoms—to choose one's attitude in any given set of circumstances, to choose one's own way."

Frankl maintained throughout his career that life can be made meaningful, even under the most dire circumstances, by what we choose to give to life and through the attitude we take toward a condition we can't change. This requires that we change habits of overly negative thinking and that we accept the fact that we are all imperfect people living in an imperfect world—a world that is made better by our good efforts and attitude.

Some pessimism is useful if it helps us avoid harmful and risky situations. Reasonable optimism does not mean sugarcoating truly bad situations. If we can avoid taking a bad job, steer clear of physical danger, refrain from making a poor investment, and get out of a bad relationship, all the better. And this sometimes requires a strong dose of skepticism in our thinking. But once these events have happened, we can make them even worse—and inhibit our ability to productively deal with them—by how we explain them to ourselves.

If we have gotten into a habit of explaining life's unpleasant events to ourselves as permanent, pervasive, and highly personal, we can enhance our well-being by changing those perspectives. The words that we express can make all the difference. Here is list of simple, common non-negative phrasing that can be used to counter unreasonably pessimistic thinking.

- "This is part of life."
- "I'll make up for it."
- "I'll get over it."
- "These things happen."
- "Everybody makes mistakes."

- "What's the worst that can happen because of this?"
- "I'll pick myself up and keep trying."
- "I just had a bad day."
- "I tried, and it just didn't work out."
- "I'll be ready next time."
- "This will pass."
- "Sometimes you win and sometimes you lose."
- "This was really bad, but I can only do what I can to make it better."
- "We're imperfect people living in an imperfect world."
- "This is unbearable. But I can keep trying by taking one small step at a time. I can choose how I will respond."

Begin to notice your explanatory style when unpleasant events happen in life. Are you unduly pessimistic? Do you have a tendency to make things seem permanent, pervasive, or overly personal? Do you make mountains out of molehills? We can all benefit by using a few handy phrases that counter unnecessary negative thinking.

SUMMARY FOR SKILL 3

Reasonable Optimism

Reasonable optimism isn't so much positive thinking as it is non-negative thinking—countering overly negative thoughts that can darken our perspective.

How we explain difficult events to ourselves shapes our attitude.

A pessimistic perspective explains setbacks as permanent, as making everything else bad, and as a negative indicator of personal worth.

A more optimistic, flexible perspective explains setbacks as temporary, as part of life, and as part of being human.

The skill of non-negative thinking requires that we discover and use phrases that can counter unduly negative thoughts that occur as we deal with the trials of everyday living.

Examples of such phrases can be found on page 30.

Figuring Out the Cash Value of Beliefs

~~~

Between believing a thing and thinking you know
is only a small step and quickly taken.

MARK TWAIN

Responding to thinking mistakes and countering non-negative thinking are two powerful tools to enhance our inner lives. However if our core mental assumptions (our beliefs) are faulty, unduly negative thoughts and feelings will continue to flow. If we carry around the core belief that life is not worthwhile, simply trying to talk back to everyday pessimistic thoughts won't be enough. We need to drill down deeper and make sure we understand and modify the beliefs that are driving those thoughts. There are four areas of belief that affect our well-being on a deep, daily basis. They are beliefs about:

1. Ourselves (self-identity)
2. Others (empathetic understanding)
3. Life (our general outlook)
4. How to behave (rules for living)

These areas of belief are the bedrock of our internal lives. They can be supportive springboards or constraining prisons. They can help us weather difficulty or subvert our hopes and dreams. But they are movable. They can be changed.

Frederick Douglass was born into slavery in the early 1800s in the state of Maryland. He was without parents by the age of ten (his father may have been a slave holder). According to his autobiography, as a young child he was taught the core belief, "God made black people to be slaves." Despite a dominant slave culture and no parental guidance, he independently came to realize that this belief system was both false and outrageously immoral. He refused to accept his identity as a slave regardless of the pressures of a larger oppressive society, which had both laws and a police state to enforce it. He defied the ban disallowing slaves to learn to read and write, and a known "slave breaker" tried to continuously beat him into submission. After two unsuccessful attempts to escape from slavery, he finally succeeded. He became a leading abolitionist, political activist, and intellectual of his day and a friend of Abraham Lincoln's. Douglass had the independence to believe what he knew was true, not what others told him. His beliefs were a strength and a springboard to his own self-regard and to personal action. He once wrote, "I would unite with anybody to do right and with nobody to do wrong."

If we have detrimental thoughts flowing through us, we can examine and defy any underlying beliefs that are supporting those thoughts. No matter how strongly those beliefs have been inculcated in us by culture or family, through conscious persistence we can choose other beliefs.

William James, the early-twentieth-century American philosopher, developed a simple rule for determining whether a belief is beneficial. He referred to it as the "cash value" of beliefs. He once wrote:

"Grant an idea or belief to be true, what concrete difference will its being true make in anyone's actual life? How will the truth be realized? What experience will be different from those which would obtain if the belief were false? What, in short, is the truth's cash-value in experiential terms?"

In other words, what good do our beliefs do us? What fruit do they produce? Do they help us or harm us? Do they make any practical difference in our lives? If they harm us, what's stopping us from changing them? Again, applying James's metaphorical phrasing: What is their cash value?

From a purely physiological perspective, beliefs are a big mystery. Somehow there is a connection between brain and mind, and this connection is somehow encoded in our genes, but we have no idea what this connection is or how it works. Mind is not physical. We can't see it or touch it. There are no color red, love of the Beatles, or algebraic calculations to be found in the cells or tissues of our brains. We therefore have no good theory about the nature of beliefs (or of any other mental causation for that matter) and no model for the exact origins of belief or of how belief and reasoning lead to choice. As Colin McGinn, the preeminent philosopher of mind, wrote in *The Mysterious Flame*:

"When billiard balls collide, they impart energy in the form of momentum to each other, and there are laws that govern this type of interaction. But beliefs and desires don't make contact with action, and there are no comparable laws governing how behavior will evolve in the causal circumstances. We simply have no general theoretical grasp of how mental states cause behavior."

We only know that as humans, beliefs are innate to us. They drive the perceptions and feelings we have of ourselves and of the world. They strongly influence what we think, how we feel, and what we do. If we believe that people should be perfect, we'll be unhappy when we and others are imperfect (which is most of the time!). If we believe that the world is mostly bad, we will live with greater fear and anxiety. If we believe we must be approved of by others, we will live our lives in conformance with others and with popular cultural beliefs and trends (whether we really want to or not).

While we may not know the physiological origins of belief, we do know something about the four factors that influence them:

1. Our natural temperament
2. How we were raised
3. Social learning
4. Our own reasoning

Sometimes it helps to understand these influences in order to understand and change beliefs that don't serve us well.

Our Natural Temperament

Our personal DNA influences our tendencies. Jerome Kagan, a developmental psychologist at Harvard University, identified at least four baseline temperamental types: timid, bold, upbeat, and melancholy. These temperaments, which can come in wide ranges of combinations, influence our beliefs. People who are naturally more timid might believe themselves less competent compared to people who are naturally more bold. People who are naturally more melancholy might have fewer hopeful beliefs than people who are more upbeat. But as Daniel Goleman, author of *Emotional Intelligence,* maintained, "Temperament is not destiny." We can mute our tendencies that don't serve us well. People who are more timid can reduce their timidity by going out of their way to participate in social opportunities. People who are naturally more melancholy can learn to consciously change habits of pessimistic thinking and engage in more activities that bring them joy.

For our well-being, it's important to try to understand our natural temperaments and to work with those tendencies that get in our way. This can in turn impact our everyday beliefs about ourselves and the world.

How We Were Raised

I was lucky enough to be raised by two loving and supportive parents. But I'm observant enough to understand that not everyone is so fortunate and that even good parents can pass along views and biases that aren't always constructive. As with everything else in life, parents and the parenting styles they use are imperfect.

In the 1960s, Diana Baumrind, a pioneering developmental psychologist at University of California, Berkeley, identified three basic styles that parents use in their approach to raising children:

1. "Authoritarian" parents impose their will in arbitrary and strict ways, allowing little autonomy or flexibility (i.e., the approach is too hard).
2. "Permissive" parents nurture but impose few limits (i.e., the approach is too soft).
3. "Authoritative" parents set limits while accepting their children's uniqueness and feelings (i.e., the approach is balanced).

Baumrind concluded that children need both warmth and limits. Without warmth it will be more difficult for them to have self-regard and empathy. Without limits, it will be more difficult for them to have self-control. Parents (and older siblings) can have a strong influence on beliefs and thinking habits by what they say and what they reward and punish (conditioning). How we view ourselves and the world today can be strongly influenced by our family experiences of the past.

The beliefs that were instilled in us by family may run so deep that we may not even be aware of what they are or of their impact. But as adults, we have the power to go back and examine these beliefs from an adult perspective. We can enlist the aid of professionals to help us examine these sometimes encrusted beliefs. At any time we can determine if childhood beliefs still make sense and, most importantly, whether they are doing us any good.

Social Learning

Peers and society at large can also influence us. From adolescence on, the influence of peers can be stronger than that of parents and family. Even if the parenting we received was mostly healthy, our larger society can influence our beliefs in ways that are not optimal. Society can communicate to us that it's not good to be uniquely who we are, that we need to conform to popular beliefs and behaviors. Consider how difficult it can be as teens to stand too far outside the mainstream of our peers with clothing and music. Our natural human "pack" tendency is to develop early loyalty to our familiar "teams" and to stay within their norms and customs.

"Social learning theory," introduced by Albert Bandura from Stanford University, is a child development model that states that children will learn many of their beliefs and behaviors from the people they observe. Children observe their parents, siblings, peers, and the larger society and make note of the types of behaviors people use and what gets rewarded and punished. Bandura's research has shown that children will imitate aggressive, altruistic, helping, and stingy models. They're more likely to imitate the behavior of people who are popular and control resources.

Social learning is quite powerful and applies to both children and adults. Our beliefs are influenced by school, friends, the media, social networks, the work place, church, and other social institutions. All of us look to our larger society to see what is considered acceptable behavior. We adopt fashions, styles, and attitudes based on what we see others doing, and we avoid whatever attracts ridicule. Beyond the possible loss of our uniqueness, there is a darker side to this imitation and conformity. Nazism, slavery, the exploitation of indigenous peoples, terrorism, and other brutal and oppressive social conditions are made possible by cultural conditions that make extremely bad behavior seem normal and acceptable.

Just as with family-based beliefs, it can be very helpful to examine the social and cultural beliefs that we've picked up and determine whether they make sense and whether they do us good. Just because our society or the unique cultures we are part of (whether ethnic, national, or religious) tell us something is okay, doesn't make it so. Douglass lived in a society in which the majority of people in power believed that slavery was acceptable—and 100 percent of those people were 100 percent terribly wrong.

Our Own Reasoning

As we humans develop over time, our learning and adult reasoning can play greater roles in our belief system. In my lifetime I have believed that Santa Claus had a fleet of helicopters; cowboys were the good guys, and Indians the bad guys; girls were not as capable as boys in sports; and more recently, with enough gumption anybody in the world could simply pick themselves up by their own "bootstraps" and accomplish whatever they want (regardless of the difficult physical body or life circumstances they were born into). But sometimes we take in new knowledge that challenges old beliefs, and sometimes we can actively review our beliefs to make sure they have cash value. According to cognitive specialists, flexibility in our thinking and a willingness to recalibrate our beliefs is quite important for our well-being. *Our own evaluation and reasoning is the path we can take to change unreasonable beliefs about self, others, and the world.*

Core beliefs are dichotomous—they categorize things as positive or negative. They help us to quickly size up people and situations. Emotions become connected to beliefs. We come to believe that some types of people, ideas, behaviors, customs, and countries are good and others are bad, and we develop an automatic good or bad feeling associated with each of those beliefs. If we develop a particularly long list of the bad, we will have negative feelings quite often.

Beliefs are also perpetuated by "confirmatory bias" and by "mental grooving." Once thoughts become beliefs, we tend to cling to evidence that confirms our beliefs and to discount evidence that contradicts them. Our beliefs become mentally grooved, acting like ruts that we quickly fall into again and again when events come up in our lives.

But we can change beliefs. Some neural connections of the brain are hardwired by the time of birth—especially those connections involved in the automatic functions of the body. But other neural connections are not hardwired; they are flexible and open to change—a condition known as "plasticity." Science says that the mind can weaken grooved neural pathways by relaxing emotional responses to old beliefs, and strengthen new ones by intentionally adopting fresh, helpful ideas.

There are many examples of individuals transforming their lives by transforming their beliefs. Queen Victoria suffered serious depression from the loss of her husband and became a recluse. But by gradually changing her perspective on life, she became a public figure dedicated to her country. Helen Keller was born deaf and blind and initially had a very negative view of life. But despite these physical limitations, she eventually developed a strong belief in herself as a person and not only learned to read and speak but she became a world-renowned author and advocate for people with disabilities. Jorge Mario Bergoglio of Argentina was a bar bouncer, a janitor, and a food chemist before a new, more-focused perspective led him to his lifelong calling to be a champion of the poor and he ultimately became Pope Francis.

The transformation of beliefs can have the miraculous effect of transforming not only individuals but entire societies. Consider the effect of changes in deep cultural beliefs on these societies:

- The warlike Vikings vs. peaceful modern-day Scandinavians
- Ancient, imperialistic Rome vs. modern egalitarian Italy
- The marauding Mongol hordes of the Middle Ages vs. the pastoral, friendly Mongolian people of modern times

The beliefs we carry as individuals and societies are profoundly important. They influence everything. Harmful beliefs lead to damaging behavior. Beneficial beliefs lead to greater well-being for individuals and societies.

Ancient writings tell us that while traveling through the village of Kesaputta, Siddhartha Gautama (the Buddha) was asked for advice regarding the teachings of the many wandering holy men in India. He gave the following sage counsel regarding hand-me-down beliefs:

"You should not go along with something because of what you have been told, because of authority, because of tradition, because of accordance with scripture ... When you know for yourselves that particular qualities are wholesome, blameless, praised by the wise, and lead to good and happiness when taken on and pursued, then you should engage in them and live by them."

Because thoughts, emotions, and behaviors flow from our core beliefs, it is important to check in and make sure we know what those beliefs are and whether they still work for us. We need to determine the cash value of our beliefs and whether they add to or subtract from our well-being. Do we have reasonable beliefs about ourselves, others, and the world—or do we have exaggerated, unreasonable core beliefs that fuel thinking mistakes, pessimism, and the unpleasant emotions and behaviors that can accompany them? If our beliefs aren't working for us, we need to consider adopting new ones.

SUMMARY FOR SKILL 4

Figuring Out the Cash Value of Beliefs

Thoughts, emotions, and behaviors flow from our fixed mental assumptions, or our core beliefs.

Reasonable beliefs can be springboards, and unreasonable beliefs can be prisons.

Given this powerful role, it's critical to make sure that our beliefs about ourselves, others, and the world are reasonable.

We do this by first examining what our beliefs are, if they contain mistakes, and what cash value they bring to our lives.

What effects, for good or ill, do they have on everyday living?

Our well-being requires that we change those unreasonable beliefs that don't serve us well.

Choosing Sensible Core Beliefs

~~~

It is wisdom to know others.
It is enlightenment to know oneself.

LAO-TZU

Steve Jobs knew from an early age that he had been adopted by his parents. When he was around seven years old, a neighborhood girl, who knew of his adoption, asked him whether his adoption meant that his real parents didn't want him. The thought startled him. He quickly ran home and with tears in his eyes asked his parents about the girl's question. His parents emphasized on that day and throughout his young life that he was especially chosen by them and a cherished member of their family. That belief made a difference for Jobs throughout the ups and downs up his dynamic life.

According to cognitive psychologists, we need a handful of simple core beliefs about ourselves, others, and the world that we can turn to through thick and thin—beliefs that provide us with a sensible perspective and keep us going. Just as with thinking mistakes, unreasonable beliefs can be based on exaggeration, labeling, and seeing only the negative.

At some point in our lives, it can be valuable to check in and make sure that our core beliefs are reasonable and healthy. If they are overly negative, they can produce additional emotional pain in our lives. If they are reasonable, they can be a powerful source of resilience.

The following sections provide some ideas about the obvious, self-evident, basic beliefs we have about self, others, and life.

Basic Beliefs about Self

A solid personal foundation of sensible core beliefs begins with a reasonable belief about self. We will struggle with happiness if we don't first accept that we are worthwhile human beings. The vast majority of us are simply regular (non-dangerous) people: above average in some ways, and below in others—we are no better or worse than anyone else.

Regular people can be any of the following:

- Rich or poor
- Pretty or homely
- Large or small
- Popular or unpopular
- Outgoing or shy
- Athletic or klutzy
- Mentally quick or mentally slow
- Foolish or wise

Only those who are chronically harmful or dangerous are *not* regular. If we've become seriously harmful or dangerous, we need to stop ourselves, get help, and change. Otherwise, we're wise to become comfortable in the skin of our own "regularness."

In line with this macro self-evident belief about self, there are corresponding micro beliefs about self that are also important for well-being. Namely, that it is entirely human to do the following:

- Make mistakes
- Be imperfect
- Be disliked or misunderstood by others

If we believe otherwise, we're out of touch with our humanity and life on this planet. We're also providing ourselves with rules that will ensure unhappiness, since there is no possible way we will be perfect or be liked and understood by everyone.

Importantly, while we're not perfect, it's also clear that the vast majority of us are capable. We can do things, and sometimes exceptionally well. Circumstances need not impede us, as exemplified by the lives of so many people from very humble beginnings such as Abraham Lincoln, Mother Teresa, and Barack Obama. We might *feel* lazy or *feel* less hopeful from time to time, but the fact is that most of us can really do things. An ongoing, unreasonable belief that says we are incapable or hopeless will imprison us with "I can't" rules, thoughts, and behaviors. We may not be able to control everything in our lives, but there is much we can do once we get started—which is sometimes the hard part. As Lao-Tzu phrased it in the ancient book the *Tao Te Ching*:

"A tree as great as a man's embrace springs from a small shoot; a terrace nine stories high begins with a pile of earth; a journey of a thousand miles starts under one's feet."

REASONABLE BELIEF ABOUT SELF

I'm a regular human being with both strengths and weaknesses.

Basic Beliefs about Others

Sometimes, in moments of impatience, it definitely feels like "I'm okay; you're not okay." Slow drivers on small roads can personally drive me crazy. But it's gradually dawned on me over time that this is so because I'm truly thinking a little crazy in those moments: I'm expecting others to be like me, I'm expecting others to understand my feelings on the road, and I'm expecting the world to be filled with "perfect" drivers who subscribe to my unique standards of speed calibration. Can't people be in a hurry like me instead of enjoying a country road? And so it goes with other areas of our lives. We do not always rationally accept others as being their own "mes," imperfect but regular. We want them to be how we want them to be, and if not, it's quite easy (and lazy) to tag them with a pejorative label.

Just like us, the majority of people in the world are simply regular—above average in some ways and below in others—with natural strengths and weaknesses. Certainly we need to identify and protect ourselves and others from people who are truly violent and cruel. We don't need to be rosy-eyed about the fact that there is real evil in the world. We need to resist and fight evil where we find it. But truly evil people are still the outliers of humanity (even though their impact can be so horribly powerful). In our everyday lives the preponderance of people are just regular. As Harper Lee wrote in *To Kill a Mockingbird*, "I think there's just one kind of folks. Folks."

If we expect others to be perfect, we will be disconnected from the actual world we are living in and will be dissatisfied with other people generally. If we believe that people should not make mistakes, we will create expectations for our children, spouses, friends, coworkers, and others that can never be met and will bring unhappiness to our relationships with them. If we have a long list of what an acceptable human being is, judgment will become a major negative force in our lives. We may overlook the positive aspects of people close to us and see only their shortcomings. If left unchecked our whole perception of society will become unreasonably dark, and our corresponding feelings filled with unnecessary negativity.

It would seem absurd to make judgments about bears, for example, in the same way that we sometimes make judgments about humans. We certainly care if a bear is rabid or dangerous, but it would seem comical if we judged a bear to be unacceptable if it had a different color of fur, had a smaller den than another, was heavier than average, was shy, learned more slowly, or made mistakes when it picked berries. Except for the really dangerous ones, bears are just bears. And people are just people.

This is not to say that we shouldn't have expectations of people's behavior at home or in the workplace or that we don't prod them to do things that need to get done. It also certainly doesn't mean that there are not consequences for all of us when we perform badly. What it does mean is that it's better for us to see the whole person rather than defining people in exaggerated and stark ways based on seeing only the bad. As Jesus taught, there is no need to focus on the splinter in someone else's eye until we've dealt with the log in our own. Overjudging others does so little good.

REASONABLE BELIEF ABOUT OTHERS

Some people are harmful and dangerous. But most people are simply regular, imperfect human beings.

Basic Beliefs about Life

As Hippocrates so aptly put it in the fourth-century BC, "Life is short, the art long, opportunity fleeting, experience treacherous, judgment difficult." The greater our expectations that life isn't supposed to be this way, the greater our inner turmoil. It's critical to our well-being to accept the nature of life and have realistic expectations of its joys, sorrows, ups, and downs. It's also critical to recognize that life requires effort. Nature teaches us that this is so for every creature on the planet, even though our natural inclination is to agree with Edgar Bergen that "hard work never killed anybody, but why take a chance?"

Like it or not, DNA ensures that each of us is born into our own unique set of challenges: physical, mental, and emotional. We are engaged in an ever-changing world of:

- Sunshine and storms
- Blossoms and thistles
- Mountain streams and raging floodwaters
- Feast and famine
- Laughter and tears
- Birth and death

Life is clearly not meant to be easy or fun all of the time, or it would be. In fact, depending upon our circumstances, life can be very painful. To think otherwise is to not see what's around us. For those who have suffered deeply, the hardened words of Westley in *The Princess Bride* likely ring true, "Life is pain. ... Anyone who says differently is selling something." We can control some things—perhaps our own choices and efforts—but there is much in life that we can't control, including the outcomes of those choices and efforts. Personal growth comes by seeing our way through difficulties and mastering ourselves in the midst of them. But sometimes, as with Victor Frankl in the Auschwitz concentration camp, there is nothing but suffering and forbearance.

But if this is all we see, then our core belief about life will be out of balance. Life also offers moments of great joy, love, humor, and fun. And as Frankl taught, our attitude and approach to life can help make the world a better place for everyone. To think that life is all drudgery can be as exaggerated as thinking it should always be easy and fun. Life is a mixture of joy and pain. As Bruce Barton wrote, "Action and reaction, ebb and flow, trial and error, change—this is the rhythm of living. Out of our overconfidence, fear; out of our fear, clearer vision, fresh hope. And out of our hope, progress."

In the end, life is as imperfect as we are—with a mixture of both joy and pain. A reasonable belief or philosophy of life most accurately sees life as it is, not solely as the perfect ideal we wish it were.

REASONABLE BELIEF ABOUT LIFE

There is both good and bad in life. I can help make the world a better place.

Basic Beliefs about Right and Wrong

Core beliefs about right and wrong—morality—are essential to both our well-being and the well-being of others. As Ralph Waldo Emerson once wrote, "By it [the moral sentiment] is the universe made safe and habitable, not by science and power." We don't need angels to come down and tell us what is right and wrong; a basic sense of right and wrong is written within the human heart.

We are born with instinctive rules of good and bad. Babies know that comfort (food, warmth, and love) is good and discomfort (hunger, pain, and lack of attention) is bad. This natural, instinctive judgment is in place for self-preservation. As humans develop and are able to be more self-managing, our sense of good and bad transcends our own self-interest and expands to the well-being of our family and others. Some people remain stuck at an infant's level of morality—only concerned about personal comfort and discomfort—but most of us are able to understand what hurts and helps others. This is the core of morality—living by rules of behavior that benefit ourselves and the world and choosing not to do things that are harmful.

Morality is an emotionally charged term, but the concept is actually simple. Morality says that some behaviors are better than others:

- Kindness is better than cruelty.
- Honesty is better than dishonesty.
- Taking care of the natural world is better than destroying it.

Sometimes moral codes can get out of hand; they can be unreasonable and excessive. Too many unnecessary rights and wrongs and too many rigid rules can lead to unhappiness. People can find themselves adopting rigid cultural rights and wrongs, involving everything from not wearing the right clothes or not being thin enough to not being in line with popular beliefs and lifestyles. The test of natural moral law is to critically and objectively ask, "What would the world be like if everyone lived by this rule?" Would it do serious harm to others or infringe unnecessarily on their freedom? Would it do unnecessary damage to our planet? Living true to natural moral law provides for the common good of all people. Or as Confucius put it so succinctly in the fifth-century BC, "Do not impose on others what you yourself do not desire."

But too little morality can be devastating, as has been demonstrated by the violent, cruel cultures of the past and present. The height of morality is simple kindness; as difficult as it can be for us humans to deliver on this simple ideal. It's good to treat others with fairness and compassion, just as we would like to be treated. It's good to wish the best for others and to have mercy. It's good to protect ourselves and others from harm and danger. Our real moral codes are the ones we live by, not the ones that we simply think or talk about. Moral beliefs are hollow without moral behavior. As the Roman philosopher Seneca once wrote, "Money may come unsought, office may be bestowed, influence and prestige may be thrust upon you, but virtue is no accident." A strong foundation for happiness is grounded in living true to core rules of right and wrong.

REASONABLE BELIEF ABOUT RIGHT AND WRONG

The world is better for us and others if we treat others as we would like to be treated.

Basic Beliefs about Personal Values

Our values include our core moral code but go well beyond morality to include everything that is of unique worth to us as individuals based on our personalities, interests, and passions. Depending on who we are, we may value family, friends, ethics, ideas, principles, community service, commerce, politics, religion, art, travel, nature, animals, and hobbies. Values have often been the core driving force in people's lives: Nelson Mandela's entire life was driven by his value of freedom for his people, Albert Einstein was driven by the personal value he placed on discovery and science, and Mother Teresa was driven by the value she placed on helping the poor.

Our lives are naturally fuller if we can discover our unique personal values and make them part of our lives. As with other beliefs, sometimes we live our lives in accordance with the values that others have passed down to us. We need to consciously decide for ourselves what *we* value. If we live our lives out of synch with these values, we will live a life that is not in congruence with who we are, and the natural result will be less happiness.

REASONABLE BELIEF ABOUT VALUES

Our values include our moral beliefs but go beyond them;
we can live more fully when we discover and live true to
what we value.

A Simple, Sensible Platform of Personal Belief

In sum then, a solid foundation for well-being requires that we have sensible, baseline beliefs. Thinking mistakes, and their corresponding unpleasant emotions and behaviors, can flow from deeper, flawed beliefs. Our well-being is enhanced by using the power of thought to transform unreasonable beliefs about ourselves, others, and life into more reasonable ones that help you build a new personal platform of beliefs.

Below are examples of unreasonable core beliefs and more reasonable alternatives.

EXAMPLES OF MORE SENSIBLE BELIEFS

UNREASONABLE BELIEF	REASONABLE BELIEF
"I'm not worthwhile (or I'm the greatest thing ever)."	"I'm a regular human being with both strengths and weaknesses."
"I'm powerless."	"I can't control everything, but there's much that I can do."
"People are bad."	"Some people are harmful and dangerous, but most people are regular, just like me."
"Life is terrible."	"There is both good and bad in the world. I can make the world a better place."
"Life should be easy and fun."	"There is both fun and difficulty in life. Life requires effort."
"I should be able to do whatever I want."	"The world is better for everyone if we treat others as we would like to be treated."

A strong platform of personal belief rests on assumptions that are believable, self-evident, and in line with common sense. To be transformative, beliefs do not need to be complicated or overly positive. "I'm the best thing ever" is just as unreliable as "I'm not worthwhile." On the contrary, the more commonsensical and believable our core beliefs, the greater their potential to be anchors in our lives and the easier it will be to quickly refer to them through thick and thin.

If we find ourselves with ongoing unhappy thoughts and feelings, we may need to take a look at our underlying core beliefs about self, others, and life:

- Are we holding on to any unreasonable core beliefs like those listed on page 57?
- Are our beliefs beneficial to us? Do they add to our well-being?
- If a friend had our current core beliefs, would we think they made sense?
- What do we value most when we really take the time to think and feel about it? Are we living our lives in synch with those values?

SUMMARY FOR SKILL 5

Choosing Sensible Core Beliefs

To enhance our well-being, we need a solid bedrock of sensible beliefs about ourselves, others, and the world that gives us strength and support through the ups and downs of life.

At a minimum, value-added core beliefs need to confirm the basic self-evident truths that:

1. we are regular, worthwhile human beings with both strengths and weaknesses,
2. some people are harmful and dangerous, but most people are just regular,
3. there is both good and bad in the world, and we can make the world a better place, and
4. the world is a better place when we treat others as we would like to be treated.

Whatever our beliefs are or become, they will have more relevance to our lives if we take the time to think about them and to choose them for ourselves rather than have others choose them for us.

Working through Diehard, Nonsensible Beliefs

~~~

It is important to know you can choose to feel good.
Most people don't think they have a choice.

NEIL SIMON

One of Frederick Douglass's lifelong friends was Susan B. Anthony. Anthony was born in 1820 and as a Quaker was an ardent antislavery advocate. Douglass would often go to the Anthony home in New York state as part of a group of key abolitionist leaders who routinely gathered to organize their efforts.

But in addition to the abolition of slavery, Anthony also took great interest in the issue of women's rights. She supported the "radical" view in her time that all humans—male and female— should have equal rights. It seems rather incredible to us now, but it was not until 1920 (after Anthony had died) that women in the United States were given the right to vote. It seems irrational to us that women could not serve on juries or take out credit in their own names. It seems extremely unjust to us that for millennia, women were considered the "property" of their fathers or husbands, like a cow or a piece of land.

From a purely reasoning perspective, how was this unequal treatment of women justified? Weren't women biologically, mentally, and emotionally fully human? Were they a different species? What was the basis for these irrational, nonsensible beliefs? Belief in the inferiority of women was based on emotionally ingrained traditions that were reinforced and passed on from generation to generation by the people in power. They were based on a false core belief that "women were not regular human beings—they were somehow less."

Even in our more enlightened times, if we're not careful, we can hold the same type of false beliefs about ourselves and others—that we are not regular human beings and somehow we are something less. We may have learned from family, peers, or our larger popular culture that people are not as good if they make mistakes, are shy, smoke, don't get good grades, are not athletic, don't have lots of friends, don't look like models, or don't wear the right clothes, among many other things. Our list of what is "bad" may simply be way too long. We may be carrying around overstuffed bags of beliefs that are full of the self-defeating "old pants and underwear" of judgment and perfectionism. We may have held these beliefs for so long that they became infused with strong emotions that don't die easily. We can begin the process of working on diehard, nonsensible beliefs by doing some unlabeling.

Unlabeling

According to cognitive specialists, one of the keys to overturning unhelpful diehard beliefs is to undo labels and to stop using them. We are not truly liberated—female or male—until we are free from unreasonable labels. As human beings we have an instinctive urge to make judgments, which can be very useful in quickly sizing up danger. But if our belief system is made up of too many simplistic judgmental labels, our inner life and our relationships can be negatively impacted. To enhance our well-being, we need to shift from beliefs based on inflexible judgmental *labels* to beliefs based on reasonable *descriptions*. As examples of the difference between these two, our beliefs can choose between:

- **Cats** = furry animals (reasonable description)
  Cats = bad (judgmental label)

- **Overweight** = more weight than desired (reasonable description)
  Overweight = bad (judgmental label)

- **Another's religion** = well-meaning, different from my own (reasonable description)
  Another's religion = heretical, demented (judgmental label)

Undoing counterproductive labels requires identifying them and returning to simple, self-evident observations. The table on page 64 provides some examples.

Again, the key to unlabeling is to move from judgmental labels to reasonable descriptions. This movement can happen through the power of thought, but it can also take time. We have been labeling things emotionally since we were infants. Our everyday experiences have prompted us to quickly label ordinary things as good or bad. People in our social world may have also influenced our development of emotionally oriented labels—by what they taught us and how they treated us. But as adults we have the chance to move beyond emotion-based beliefs to see if they hold up in the light of day, to see how they hold up when compared to reasonable descriptions.

UNLABELING

BELIEFS BASED ON JUDGMENTAL LABELS	UNLABELING USING REASONABLE DESCRIPTIONS
"He doesn't like me. There must be something wrong with me."	"It's not pleasant to be disliked, but I'm just a regular person whether I'm liked by everyone or not."
"I really screwed up; I'm a failure."	"Messing up on something is just messing up; it doesn't magically change a person into a failure."
"My friend was inconsiderate; he's a jerk."	"My friend isn't a jerk; he's just a regular, imperfect person."
"Several people were killed in that earthquake; life is terrible."	"Life is filled with both joy and pain. We live in an imperfect world and sometimes horrible things happen."
"My life is as boring as hell; life sucks."	"Life is both fun and difficult. I need to apply effort if I want something new to happen."

Socratic Method

Sometimes to help uproot unreasonable beliefs that have become emotionally ingrained, it can help to use the Socratic method—to ask ourselves questions that can make problems with our beliefs more obvious.

Socrates was born in the city of Athens in 469 BC and died there in 399 BC. He was a stonemason who also served in the Athenian army. He eventually settled into a life of teaching and philosophical discussion, and his passion was to test the common everyday beliefs of his society, especially the ones that he believed did not make sense or led to unhappiness. He once asked, "And if someone merely asserts that something is so, are we going to concede that it is so? Or are we going to examine what the speaker says?"

His method was to ask simple questions, and he believed underlying beliefs could be found in the answers. He kept asking these questions on deeper levels until he got down to the core beliefs. He was interested in the worth (cash value) of beliefs. This Socratic method is the same technique that cognitive specialists use to help people look at beliefs that may be causing them unnecessary, unhappy feelings. It is examining our own assertions with very basic questions such as the following:

- "Why would that be true?"
- "Why would that be bad (even if it were true)?"
- "Who made that rule?"
- "Does this belief make sense?"
- "Does it do me any good?"

When we are feeling unnecessarily unhappy too often, it can help to seek out the beliefs behind our thinking to see if they make sense and do us any good. Just as Susan B. Anthony was able to see the obvious truth that women were not less than men, we need to make sure that our own personal core beliefs are just as sensible.

Socratic questioning can help us in this endeavor. We can either do this mentally or by writing things down, but the key is to make note of bothersome thoughts, ask simple probing questions, and drill down a few layers until we get to the assumptions (beliefs) behind those patterns of thought. Ultimately we can identify more reasonable beliefs that can be referred to in the future in similar situations. Here are a few examples of the Socratic method for uncovering unreasonable beliefs:

Feeling That You Are a Bad Person for Telling a "Dumb" Story

Thought: "I'm a complete idiot for telling that story."
Question: "Why would that be true?"
Thought: "Because it was a dumb story and made me look dumb."
Question: "Why would that be bad?"
Thought: "Because it's bad to look like an idiot."
Questions: "Is this really true? Who made it true? Does it do me any good?"

MORE SENSIBLE BELIEF

"I'm a bad person if I'm a psycho killer, not if I tell a dumb story. I'm just a regular human."

Refusing to Forgive Someone for Hurting Your Feelings

Thought: "She really hurt my feelings; I'll never speak to her again."
Question: "Why not?"
Thought: "Because you can't forgive people who say really mean things about you."
Questions: "Is this really true? Who made it true? Does it do me any good?"

MORE SENSIBLE BELIEF

"People make mistakes, and people can make up and forgive each other if they choose."

Can't Find Work, So I'm Not Going to Try Anymore

Thought: "I can't find work, so I might as well give up."
Question: "Why would giving up help me?"
Thought: "It wouldn't help me, but I can't do it anymore."
Questions: Is this really true? Does it do me any good?

MORE SENSIBLE BELIEF

"Life is sometimes hard, but I can do things
once I get started."

Beliefs are only ideas, yet emotionally they can seem completely real and true, even when they're not. And since they are ideas, they can be questioned and tested. And if they are questioned and tested and found to be untrue, they can be changed. It may take some mental effort over a sustained time period to chisel away at this embedded mental rock, but if unreasonable beliefs are causing us unhappiness, it's worth taking some time to make some improvements.

Additional Approaches to Working with Diehard Unreasonable Beliefs

Unlabeling and the Socratic method as illustrated above on pages 64–66, are two approaches that can help change unreasonable beliefs. In her book *Cognitive Behavior Therapy*, Dr. Judith Beck outlines a number of additional useful tools to help change unreasonable beliefs. The following are brief descriptions of some of these tools:

- **Examining advantages/disadvantages**—After identifying your core beliefs, write down the advantages and disadvantages of holding those beliefs. Do they help you?
- **Acting "as if"**—Force yourself to carry out behaviors that are logically reasonable even if emotionally you still

feel like they aren't (e.g., ask questions when you don't know something, go to a party even though you feel shy, state an unpopular opinion, tell people "no" even when it's hard to emotionally, etc.)

- **Cognitive continuum**—Alter unreasonable all-or-nothing beliefs about self and others by using a rational rating/scale of personal competence, effectiveness, popularity, etc., rather than a stark 0 percent or 100 percent standard (i.e., instead of saying you are 100 percent incompetent at mathematics, figure out your actual competence rating: are you 50 percent capable? Eighty percent capable?). Get more realistic and honest in your assessments of yourself and others.

- **Self-disclosure**—Expressing honest thoughts about unhappy events and feelings with others, asking if they have experienced something similar, and getting their perspectives

- **Extreme contrasts**—Compare your beliefs about self or others to extreme examples. Compare yourself or others to Hitler or Stalin. How bad are you or your irritating buddy, really? Compare yourself to an extremely harmful person you're familiar with—how do you compare? Where are you on the bell curve of humanity when it comes to harmful and dangerous?

- **Stories and metaphors**—Look to stories, people, and examples that counter unreasonable beliefs. Neither Abraham Lincoln nor Martin Luther King were liked by many people, but that did not make them less worthwhile. Albert Einstein may not have been good at basketball but that did not make him incompetent. Cinderella wasn't a problem child—she was just a regular human being—but her harsh stepmother and stepsisters made her feel otherwise.

- **Revisiting early memories**—Use your adult reasoning power to assess unreasonable things you may have been told by parents, siblings, school children, or others in the past—about yourself, others, and the world—that have led to unreasonable beliefs in the present. Speak back to these people in your mind; stand up for your child self as you would for a child of your own.

- **Coping card**—Write down and refer to reasonable beliefs and rules for living that are most relevant to you in everyday difficult situations.

All of these approaches can be facilitated by using the help of a counselor or coach trained in cognitive-behavioral therapy—someone who can help provide an objective perspective on beliefs and help provide alternative beliefs, rules for living, and ways of thinking. We use coaches and tutors for sports, academics, hobbies, physical therapy, and all matter of endeavors. Why not use one for this very important aspect of our lives if it's not all that easy for us? The bottom line is that if our beliefs affect our well-being in a negative way, we can go through the effort to make them better.

SUMMARY FOR SKILL 6

Working through Diehard Nonsensible Beliefs

Sometimes unreasonable, counterproductive beliefs do not die easily, and we need to put in some effort to identify and change them.

The first approach is to move away from beliefs based on simplistic, judgmental labels and toward beliefs based on reasonable descriptions.

Sometimes to uncover unreasonable labels and rules we are using in our lives, it can be helpful to use the Socratic method of drilling down, with simple questions, until we see the core label or rule that is driving our thinking.

Why would that be true?
Why would that be bad?
Who made that rule?
Does it do me any good?

There are many other techniques that cognitive experts use to help uncover and alter unreasonable beliefs, some of which are summarized on pages 67–69.

Solution Thinking

~~~

When you have exhausted all possibilities,
remember this—you haven't.

THOMAS EDISON

I had the good fortune of having a good friend and business part-
ner who was also a highly respected designer in his field. Perhaps
because of his natural design instincts, Bill was always in solution
mode, whether he was designing a university campus or making
decisions about our company. One learned very quickly that you
couldn't casually complain to Bill about a problem because he
would quickly pick up the phone and try to solve it with you
standing there. He hated problems to fester. With his uniquely
unabashed honesty he would be the first to admit that his solutions weren't always perfect (as if they ever could be), but he
taught me the lesson of solving problems directly before they
become bigger.

If there are real-life problems behind our emotional turmoil,
just changing our perceptions of the problems won't do. Problems
require a different power of thought: active solution thinking. One

of the clear realities of human existence is that we live in an imperfect world filled with difficulties. Problems are the challenges that stand between us and our aspirations. We don't want them, yet without them there would be little for us to do on this planet. Problems are fundamental to our human experience.

Children in ancient Greece were raised on the epic wisdom poem called the *Odyssey* (in fact, Homer's books were literally like the Bible to ancient Greeks). In the *Odyssey*, a king named Odysseus leaves Troy at the end of the Trojan war and experiences a difficult, ten-year-long journey back to his home on the island of Ithaca. He encounters storms, cannibals, monsters, dangerous magic, and human foes. He has many narrow escapes, and his journey is filled with troubles. Even upon his ultimate arrival home, he is challenged by young men who have been trying to take over his household in his absence. Greek youth were told this tale in order to impress upon them that life is like a difficult journey that requires heroic courage and perseverance.

Heroic tales have application still. Each of us is on our own unique journey. We are beset by problems large and small on a daily basis. We can worry and ruminate over problems (and let them fester), or we can take them on as the natural challenges of our life journey. If we have serious addictions, financial difficulties, damaged personal relationships, a community that is unsafe or unhealthy, or simply need to figure out what to do with our lives, changing our perspective won't be enough. We need to slay our monsters and steer through our storms.

In his book *Thinking Fast and Slow*, Daniel Kahneman documents the fact that we humans approach problems either through faster, intuitive means (thinking fast) or slower, analytical means (thinking slow). Thinking fast works fine for a lot of everyday situations, but it can be faulty when it comes to more complicated problems. There are a lot of natural built-in biases with thinking fast, and it's easy to jump to solutions without considering all of the factors. Since we're trying to make decisions quickly, it's easy to skip important information. "Solution thinking" requires us to slow down and rather than automatically going with the quickest, easiest solution that comes to mind, take the time to ask ourselves a few questions and explore the options. Solution thinking involves asking ourselves the following questions:

- "What's the real problem?"
- "What's a good target solution?"
- "What's the strategy to accomplish the target solution?"
- "What are the weekly/daily to-do items needed to carry out the strategy?"

Solution thinking is actively shifting gears when we have problems and consciously *thinking* through problems and solutions. Simple problems usually can be resolved with simple, intuitive solutions, but for more difficult problems, even brief solution thinking can make a difference.

Real Problems

Solution thinking steps back from immediate problems and asks more broadly, "What do I really need to accomplish?" Sometimes we can quickly work on one problem without thinking too much about it, only to discover that our *real* problem is something else—often something bigger. It's often helpful to back up and look at larger purposes. For example:

- Immediately trying to figure out which college to go to, when we first need to decide what work we want to do for a living and whether we even need a college education
- Immediately trying to get out of a relationship, when we first need to decide if this person is someone we

truly care about and ideally want in our lives, and if we can try to improve communication and make changes on our side to improve the relationship

- Immediately trying to figure out how to hide our drug problem from our children, when we more critically need to figure out how to best get the help we need to overcome our addiction

Odysseus's larger purpose wasn't how to defeat a Cyclops but how best to return to his home and family in Ithaca.

Target Solutions

Once we've determined what our real problem is (i.e., what we really need to accomplish), we're in a better position to discover a good solution. The chemist and author Linus Pauling once wrote, "The best way to have a good idea is to have lots of them." And so it is with solutions. To discover a target solution, it's helpful to first think through a bunch of options, especially when it comes to big problems. Generating a well-considered target solution requires both brainstorming and assessment.

BRAINSTORMING This is taking the mental effort to open up our minds to possibilities; to not just taking the first few ideas that naturally and quickly come to us, but to prod our intuitions further (see *The Care and Feeding of Ideas* by James Adams). The following are a few steps that can be taken to prompt a more robust brainstorming process:

- Jot down or draw on paper your initial solutions without concern for spelling, complete sentences, precise drawings, erasing, or anything else—just having fun with ideas
- Ignore fear, confusion, and other emotional inhibitors as background noise

- Include off-the-wall solutions, since the more obvious ones will always be ready at hand
- Talk to and learn from others who have had actual experience with the problem area
- Expand your knowledge by looking at ideas on the internet and in libraries, books, and magazines and by talking to industry associations, as well as testing out ideas in practice
- List any and all solution ideas (perhaps something like the following)

  ▸ Real problem: Make a living over the next few years at something I enjoy and care about
  ▸ Solution brainstorm list:
    ✔ Join the Army
    ✔ Join the Peace Corps
    ✔ Work at a surf shop in Hawaii
    ✔ Start a Google ad-consulting business
    ✔ Start a longer-term career path to solve my longer-term living aspirations; plan it out
    ✔ Join the circus

ASSESSMENT Once we've opened up our minds to possibilities through brainstorming, we need to select a solution alternative. Rather than solely going with a gut feeling, it can help to test our gut feeling against a rational assessment—even if very simple:

- After brainstorming, consider the pluses and minuses of your top solution options
- You can use a simple "Ben Franklin balance sheet" (as follows on the next page)

"BEN FRANKLIN" BALANCE SHEET

OPTION	PLUSES	MINUSES
Joining the Army	✔ Stable income ✔ Benefits ✔ Training ✔ See the world ✔ Pension	✔ Rules/authority ✔ Could get killed
Joining the Peace Corps	✔ Help people ✔ Live abroad ✔ Learn/tour ✔ Living expenses covered ✔ Consistent with key values	✔ Financially unstable ✔ Away from home
Joining the circus	✔ Really fun ✔ Make kids happy ✔ Lots of travel ✔ Tattoos	✔ Financially unstable ✔ Love life suffers

- For really big decisions, you can drill down even further and look at key factors to assess a solution:

  ▸ Benefits—What will be the positive outcomes from the solution?

  ▸ Requirements—What will need to be done?

  ▸ Costs—How much money will be required?

  ▸ Risks—What are the worst things that could happen? Is there any way to minimize risks by modifying the solution or having a Plan B?

- You can use a solutions rating chart

SOLUTIONS RATING CHART

RATING CATEGORY*	JOINING THE ARMY	JOINING THE PEACE CORPS	JOINING THE CIRCUS
Benefits			
• Income	6	3	5
• Enjoyment	5	7	10
Requirements	5	5	5
Cost	8	8	6
Risks			
• Financial	7	4	5
• Safety	2	5	5

★ If one factor is more important than another, they can be weighted accordingly; for example, if Factor A is twice as important as Factor B, multiply Factor A by two.

Rating: 10 = really good; 1 = really bad

The books *Smart Choices* by John Hammond, Ralph Keeney, and Howard Raiffa and *Breakthrough Thinking* by Gerald Nadler and Shozo Hibino provide additional example of solution generation and evaluation tools.

Until we figure out which target we want to sail toward, we might find ourselves sailing through stormy waters in the wrong direction. If we've gotten off course or don't know where we are, identifying target solutions can help us chart a new course.

Strategy

Determining a target solution is critical to making sure we're solving the right problem or aiming in the right direction, but alone it's not enough. We also need to carry out the right effort, or *strategy*. A target solution answers *what*, and a strategy answers *how*.

- If my target career solution is to be an airline pilot, I need to determine my strategy for getting the necessary qualifications and, eventually, a job.
- If my target family solution is to spend more time with my children, I need to determine how I'm going to make it happen.
- If my target community solution is to have less crime in my neighborhood, I need to determine the most likely strategy to employ to really make a difference.

We naturally, intuitively generate strategies all the time—from major decisions on how to find a job or how to deal with a child's drug problem to what moves to make in a poker game. But for some of the most important decisions in our lives, we sometimes don't take the time to research and think sufficiently about all the options. As with identifying target solutions, we can use our creativity to list a variety of strategies by applying the same elements of brainstorming and assessment. Once again, it can be helpful to think about the least obvious strategies because the most obvious will always be at hand. It can be especially helpful to keep an eye open for approaches that are simple and inexpensive as first-step experiments. From small test-pilot experiments with strategy we can learn what works best for reaching our target solution.

To-Do Items

The last step of developing a solution—turning the solution plan into weekly or daily tasks— is crucial. If specific tasks aren't written down as to-do items on a daily schedule, they may not happen. Solutions aren't solutions until they're implemented. We ultimately need to write down daily tasks, schedule them on a calendar, prioritize them, and jump in and do them. We need to make phone calls, appointments, and any payments or other commitments that put our "skin" in the game even when we don't feel like it. Solutions, at the end of the day, require action.

Once we've determined a target solution and a strategy, we have the ingredients for a simple solution plan, as shown on page 80.

We come up with simple solution plans intuitively in our heads all the time. We have this natural solution-thinking ability within us. Getting into the habit of solution thinking is transformative not only because it produces solutions, but also because it steers us away from the mental churning that can produce emotional turmoil.

SOLUTION PLAN EXAMPLE

Real problem	How to make a living (or at least cover my costs) over the next few years so I can do something I enjoy and care about
Target solution	Join the circus (joining the Peace Corps is Plan B)
Strategy	• List out all circus and related companies • Get information from major circus companies • Do more research on type and supply/demand for circus jobs over next ten years • Network my way into conversations • Get advice from circus employees • Get a job directly with major US or non-US circus companies • Go to the National Circus School (if there's not less-expensive, direct route)
Daily to-do items	• Using the strategy as a guide, reserve one to two hours each day to carry out strategy tasks. Write down the most important to-do items at the beginning of each day

Solutions to Conflict Problems

As we all know, conflict is a special kind of problem. It's a problem in which people contend with each other to get what they want. Some conflict is natural and normal. If different people want different things, they may stand up strongly for what they want or believe in. And if people want something that's really important to them, sometimes they have to go through some struggle to get it. However, if conflict happens too often, is too mean, or becomes an easy habit, it can be very corrosive. War is the extreme example of how terrible conflict can be. Peace is what comes when we learn to talk through and solve our differences rather than fight over them.

When conflict arises, we need to stop and consciously take a time-out from arguing with each other, and instead take a "time-in" toward the solution. Becoming solution-minded can help us to become more effective in getting important things done but can also help maintain stronger relationships. My father's humble Idahoan parents had the simple habit of sitting down at the kitchen table to discuss problems as they arose rather than going through the emotional outbursts that couples sometimes experience. This discussions-at-the-kitchen-table image is a good symbol for reducing the amount of unnecessary conflict in our lives, especially with those closest to us.

The compelling principle-based concepts coming out of the Harvard Negotiation Project of the 1980s are summarized in the classic book, *Getting to Yes*, written by professors Roger Fisher and William Ury. Some of the most helpful approaches emerging from the project regarding dealing with conflict/negotiations include the following:

- Separate the people from the problem. In dealing with conflict, it helps to first understand the perceptions and feelings of the other person. It's critical to not get defensive, take things personally, blame people, or respond to emotional outbursts with additional angry words, and it's important to seek to understand how people feel while also expressing how you feel and to get perceptions and emotions out on the table. People are emotional beings and conflict is made worse by not first consciously empathizing with people and understanding their perceptions and feelings.

- Focus on interests rather than positions. Rather than digging into assumed positions on a problem, discuss each side's interests. List out what each party wants or needs. Keep asking questions to ensure that those interests are well understood and well justified. *Be hard on the problem and soft on the people.* In the end, make sure that interests are expressed with detail and clarity to ensure that they're reasonably justified.

- Work together to create options that will satisfy both parties (win-win). Once interests are clearly understood, embark on brainstorming to create solutions that meet the interests of both parties. Create and look at as many options as possible. For a solution to work, both parties need to have some interests met. This likely means compromise—not everyone gets exactly what he or she wants, but all the parties get at least something they want. If the solution only benefits you, the solution is likely to be short-lived and cause other problems down the road. Unless we're talking about opposing serious harm, getting only what you want is usually the antithesis of a principle-based, fair resolution of conflicts.

- Don't allow for power plays or other game playing. Sometimes people don't want a reasonable resolution. They either actually *want* conflict (it's personal and about you, not about the problem) or they simply want their own way and feel like they can bulldoze everyone else to get it. They're not interested in compromise. If you have made your case as objectively and clearly as possible and have tried to meet legitimate interests on both sides through compromise, then it's time to try to engage an independent referee (friend, counselor, mediator, judge) to help mediate a solution. Or it's time to walk away and go with the best available alternative solutions that meet your needs and interests.

Whether conflict or other types of problems, we can transform our own situations and our world by using the power of thought to engage in a more solution-thinking approach to living.

Key Problem-Solving Questions

- "What is the real problem?"
- "What are the possible solutions?"
- "What are the possible strategies to achieve my target solution?"
- "What tasks will I do this week?"

Key Conflict Problem-Solving Questions

- "How does each party *feel* about the problem?"
- "What are each party's reasonable interests?"
- "What solutions will help meet at least some of the interests of each party?"
- "If one party chooses to simply try to use power or bullying—or if parties simply can't see eye to eye—who can be used as an independent referee? Or is it time to walk away?"

SUMMARY FOR SKILL 7

Solution Thinking

If there are real-life problems behind worry and emotional unease, just changing our perception of events won't be sufficient. We need to switch gears and get into an active solution-thinking mode.

For everyday problems, quick, intuitive solutions can be just fine, but for moderate to important problems, it can be helpful to slow down and consider other factors and options.

Solution thinking involves (1) determining what our real problem is (based on what we really need to accomplish), (2) identifying target solutions, (3) determining strategies to carry out a target solution, and (4) carrying out daily tasks (to-do items) in order to accomplish our solution.

In addition, for solving conflict problems, it can be helpful to (1) get emotions out on the table (understand how conflicted parties feel), (2) understand each party's reasonable interests, (3) identify solutions that address the interests of the parties (compromise), and (4) bring in an intermediary (a referee of some kind) if one party does not want to compromise or if the interests are not reconcilable.

Upgrade Your Mood by Jumping In

~~~

If you wait for the perfect moment, when all is safe and assured, it may never arrive. Mountains will not be climbed, races won, or lasting happiness achieved.

MAURICE CHEVALIER

Directly changing distorted self-defeating thoughts—and the beliefs that sustain them—is an important approach to enhancing our internal well-being. But the second element of cognitive behavioral therapy, activating behavior, is equally important. One ongoing University of Washington study indicates that behavior activation can actually be more effective in helping people with depression than purely cognitive approaches. Thoughts can change feelings and behavior, but behavior can also influence feelings and thoughts. When we do something we naturally enjoy, complete a necessary task, or perform an act of kindness, pleasant emotions and thoughts often accompany our efforts.

Jumping in and taking action when we don't feel like it emotionally (or behavior activation, in more technical terminology) can be an important tool in reenergizing our sense of well-being if we have become immobilized by negative emotions. According to behavioral psychologists, two helpful antidotes to anxiety and depression are general activity and exercise (as able). Avoiding physical activity can sometimes go beyond simple rest and relaxation and spill into avoidance behavior—avoiding work, relationships, emotional discomfort, or perceived threats. *Jumping in* is working from the outside-in. We enhance our inner well-being by engaging in productive activity in spite of our moods.

Mike Wallace, the famous CBS newsman, spent several years suffering with depression but was ashamed to acknowledge it. He viewed it as a stigma rather than as an illness not of his own choosing. He got to the point where he couldn't eat or sleep and he shut down his life. In 1982 he attempted suicide and was saved only by having his stomach pumped of sleeping pills, and subsequently by his wife jumping in and taking quick action to help in his recovery. He received professional help and medication. He also started to exercise, returned to active work, and began to do recreational activities even when he didn't feel like it. He experienced more than twenty years of additional productive living through jumping in (actually being *pushed in* by his wife) and taking action in the midst of his emotional disability. The lesson from his life experience should not be trivialized for anyone dealing with chronic emotional pain. Activity was one key element that helped him to ultimately cope with depression, but he also received the help he needed from health professionals, medication, and the strong support of family and friends. All of these were necessary for his recovery.

There are lots of things we need to do in life. We need to work at jobs, carry out everyday chores, take care of others, go to school, deal with our own health requirements, maintain relationships, and so on. There may also be many things that we want to do to make our lives even more full, such as helping people in need, learning new skills, developing talents, meeting new people, engaging in recreational pursuits, and taking on new and interesting challenges. All of these are only possible by taking action, regardless of our moods.

When we need to do things that aren't fun or seem threatening, it's normal to have thoughts come to us that say, "I can't" or "It's too hard." It's also normal to have these kinds of thoughts when we have to do new things that worry us (finding a new job, meeting new people, or having an elderly parent become seriously ill). But we also have the power inside of us to respond to "I can't" thoughts and to take action regardless of the natural emotions that may keep us from acting. Effort may not always be easy or fun, but it usually is not nearly as hard as our thoughts and feelings can make it seem.

"But Twists"

In order to help get ourselves started, we can counter the "I can't," "I won't," "I don't want to," or "It's too hard" thoughts with quick rebuttals, something that I've referred to as "but twists" in previous books. A "but twist" is a response to words that are not helpful with a more constructive "but" phrase. For example, if we say to ourselves, "Filling out this resume is so hard; I don't want to do it," some but twists would be: "… but I can just get started and see how it goes" or "… but I can get help on the internet if I need it" or "… but the sooner I get it the done, the sooner I can use it" or "… but it won't kill me." The point of the but twist, or similar mental tool, is to use a few quick words just to get us started. If we wait until we *feel* like doing something we need to do, we may never do it. Behavioral specialists maintain the obvious point that activity breeds more activity, and inactivity breeds more inactivity. Action often precedes motivation. As Meryl Streep succinctly put it, "Start by starting."

Here are some additional examples of common but twists that can help us talk back to and let go of helpless "I can't" thoughts:

- ". . . but I can do it"
- ". . . but it's really not that hard"
- ". . . but it really won't take very long"
- ". . . but I can just take one small step at a time"
- ". . . but it'll be great to have done it"
- ". . . but it won't kill me"
- ". . . but I'm really just having a feeling about it—I'll just jump in and see how hard it really is"
- ". . . but I can just start and see how it goes"
- ". . . but I can get help if it gets too hard"

Daily Activity Lists

Taking needful actions when we don't feel like it can have the additional benefit of changing our beliefs about our capability to get things done. It provides test-case examples of doing. For instance:

- If we perform an act of kindness when we don't feel like it, we learn that we can be patient and helpful even when it's not easy.
- If we do the dishes when we feel lazy, we learn we can get things done even when we don't want to.
- If we jump in and do things that are difficult for us and then keep picking ourselves up if we fail, we develop first hand knowledge about our own resilience and determination.

One of the key tools that behavioral specialists use to help people who have become inactive due to strong anxiety or depression is to help them develop daily activity schedules. Without clear, written, prioritized lists, activity can seem overwhelming. Breaking daily tasks down into small, easily accomplished actions can activate behavior. Included in the schedule are at least a few activities that are (1) personally enjoyable and (2) demonstrate a basic level of self-mastery. The activity rule that becomes emphasized for people in this mode is "When feeling blue, get active" rather than "When feeling blue, shut down." It is recognizing that the inactivity rule doesn't have much cash value if somebody has things that they need to do in their everyday lives.

Winston Churchill is known for his extraordinary leadership during World War II, but what isn't always appreciated is that Churchill did this in spite of a history of deep anxiety. He stuttered as a child, was bullied, did poorly in school, and was given very little parental attention or affection growing up. In his thirties he complained to his friends that he was hounded by the "black dog" of depression. As he sat in the houses of the British Parliament he would sometimes contemplate suicide. His "black dog" followed him through much of his life. Despite this serious affliction, he was a man of action who changed the course of history. He led his country and Western Europe through unparalleled military and political battles. He jumped into action in spite of his dark moods. Think of the difference Churchill made in the lives of others because he kept going even when he didn't feel like it. As he once said, "When you're going through hell, keep going."

The following are lessons from behavioral specialists for all of us:

- Our efforts can easily be thwarted by our natural emotions. In cases when we have important things to get done, it's essential to acknowledge and accept our emotions in those instances for what they are—natural unpleasant emotional sensations, or "noise." When there are things to be done, we need to simply jump into activity because so much of the time *motivation comes after activity, not before it.* Sometimes we need to let that emotional noise play on as we would an unpleasant commercial on the radio. We don't choose these emotions; they come to us as part of our imperfect bodies, so if that noise is particularly uncomfortable and disrupting our lives, then we need to jump in and get help from health professionals just as we would if we had a physical ailment that was immobilizing us. As Tennessee Williams once wrote, "Make voyages! Attempt them! There is nothing else."

- Being confused about what to do can lead to anxiety and inaction. Maintaining a simple, prioritized, daily to-do list can help us remember and organize the activities we want and need to do.

- Beyond doing the things we need to get done, we can integrate more of what we simply enjoy into our everyday lives and do less of what is naturally stressful to us. At least a few of our everyday to-do items should be fun and easy.

SUMMARY FOR SKILL 8

Upgrade Your Mood by Jumping In

While changing our thinking can influence our emotional well-being, our behavior is equally important.

When we do something we naturally enjoy, complete a necessary task, or perform an act of kindness, we often experience pleasant emotions and thoughts.

Jumping in means doing things in our lives even when we don't feel like it—in spite of our imperfect emotions.

Behavioral specialists maintain that people who have a natural tendency toward "I can't" emotions need to follow the activity rule of "When feeling blue, get active."

Using quick rebuttals, or "but twists," to respond to "I can't" or "It's too hard" thoughts can help in getting started.

Specialists also maintain that having simple, daily to-do lists that include a few fun and easy tasks can help activate behavior and keep us from getting overwhelmed.

Action often precedes motivation—not vice versa.

Choosing Your Big Worldview: Cosmic Beliefs

~~~

*Since I cannot believe that this was the result of chance,
I have to admit to anti-chance. And so I must believe in a
guiding power in the Universe.*

JANE GOODALL

One day my wife and our son Jackson (who was then eight years old) were riding along in our car, and Jackson was looking out the window, deep in thought. Finally he turned to my wife and said, "I've got two really big questions: first of all, where did Payless Drugs get its name and second, where did God come from?" It goes without saying that the first question was much easier to deal with than the second. These simple questions exemplify in a nutshell the position we find ourselves in as human beings. In the midst of our everyday, mundane world we miraculously have the capacity to be aware of and contemplate the much larger universe. We are not only self-conscious and other-conscious, but we also experience "cosmic consciousness": an awareness of the larger universe and our place in it.

Just as with other beliefs in our lives, these "cosmic beliefs" can be helpful to us or they can weigh us down; they can be reasonable or unreasonable. Regardless of the content of our beliefs, the "fruits" of these beliefs are most constructive if they bring us greater well-being. Until we come to terms with and fully accept (without ongoing tumult) our "big picture" beliefs about the universe and life, we are likely to experience expanded emotional pain during the most difficult and tragic times of our lives.

Whether or not our big worldviews include a belief in an intentional, purposeful universe, there are certain concepts that seem reasonably fundamental:

- We are in the midst of eternity.
- Several very specific laws and forces have come together to make the universe and life possible.
- According to modern quantum physics, reality at the unobserved, subatomic level is immaterial—made up of immaterial waves of information and potential.
- We experience the world and our inner lives solely through our minds (even our physical sensations must pass through our minds before we experience them).
- We are thus mental beings experiencing a physical existence that is seemingly immaterial at its most fundamental level.
- For those so inclined, there is justification for the famous quote of Pierre Teilhard de Chardin, "We are not human beings having a spiritual experience; we are spiritual beings having a human experience."

Our big-picture beliefs are important to us, but they are also constrained. As the German philosopher Immanuel Kant argued so convincingly over two hundred years ago, we are unable to know the truth with a capital T. We know our own personal mental experience, but we don't know what kind of knowledge lies beyond this experience. The universe as we experience it does not exist independently of our unique mental faculties. In the arena of science, we know if a scientific theory is successful or not by it being testable and repeatable, but we don't know if it contains ultimate Truth. Our personal mental experience tells us that the law of gravity successfully predicts that apples fall to the ground, but we don't know what gravity really is or where it comes from outside of that mental experience. No matter what assumptions we make about the universe, they are ultimately based on faith.

The universe has gifted us humans with the physical senses of sight, taste, smell, touch, and hearing, but we are also born with the very real, nonphysical senses of reason, morality, love, joy, beauty, humor, and faith. We are born with a sense of awe and wonder. Our basic capacity to believe in things, and have hope, is inborn—it needs no more justification for its existence than does our capacity to reason, to communicate, to play music, or to create a poem.

In the realm of religion, human beings do not simply believe in prayer, meditation, faith, repentance, or a sense of something greater than themselves—humans are born with the capacity to naturally *experience* these spiritual and religious influences. Some people feel an emotional/spiritual connection to the "more" of the universe when they are out in nature or looking up at the stars, while others feel it when they pray, meditate, or sit in a sacred place. As William James documents in his classic work *The Varieties of Religious Experience*, this spiritual sense has been experienced and ritualized in various ways through time, but it seems to be held in common by much of humanity. And just as with our physical senses, what our inner senses enjoy and respond to can be quite different from one person to another. As the Dalai Lama wrote in *The Art of Happiness*:

"In this world, there are so many different people, so many dispositions. … I believe that each individual should embark upon a spiritual path that is best suited to his or her mental disposition, natural inclination, temperament, belief, family, and cultural background. Now, for example, as a Buddhist monk, I find Buddhism most suitable. But that does not mean that Buddhism is best for everyone. That's clear. It's definite. If I believed that Buddhism were best for everyone, that would be foolish, because different people have different mental dispositions."

Is the universe the result of chance or nonchance? Which seems like the more reasonable explanation and which belief gives us the most cash value? The laws of nature are not based on random numbers but on highly specific numbers and properties that come together in precise ways to make the universe and life possible. There are thought to be more than 200 precise parameters that had to be just right in the universe for humans to exist, which seems to make chance a highly implausible explanation. Any belief must account for this finely tuned reality and for the rich immaterial reality (the spirit) of inner human experience. On the other hand, we find ourselves in a world filled with sorrow, evil, and death, controlled by these same unbending laws of nature. Any belief must account for this as well. Regardless of our larger beliefs, it's clear that for a short period of time, we are compelled to experience an imperfect mortal life that includes both uncertainty and suffering.

There is no need to make our faith in these macro beliefs too rigid. Dogmatic beliefs can needlessly engender unhappiness for us and others. Fundamentalism in all its forms, both theistic and atheistic, has led to times of great human tragedy (consider the crusades of Christianity, the jihads of Islam, and the persecution and attempted eradication of religion by Marxist dictators). The fruits of inflexible, dogmatic fundamentalism have proven to be bitter for humankind.

Additionally, people are sometimes so fundamentally focused on not making errors in their beliefs, that they reject all belief that isn't completely certain (as if it ever could be). By being so intellectually strict, people can lose out on important beliefs and experiences that might bring them greater happiness. It is, as William James pointed out, not unlike the bachelor who is in love but chooses not to marry in order to ensure that he doesn't make a mistake. It's true that he will eliminate all uncertainty by not marrying, but he also risks missing out on some of the most wonderful possibilities of his life. A belief that isn't 100 percent certain may still be extremely valuable if it's believable *enough* and brings happiness and goodness to our lives.

Martin Luther King once wrote of how in his youth "doubts began to spring forth unrelentingly." He was the son of a Christian minister, and he shocked his conservative Sunday school class when at the age of thirteen he announced his doubts about the bodily resurrection of Jesus. Later, in college, he developed a faith that made sense and worked for him—to the point of his being comfortable enough to become a minister himself. He developed a faith and worldview that sustained him throughout his adult life and that ultimately inspired him to help change the world. He did not take an all-or-nothing position on key big-picture issues.

For many people, a core belief in an ultimate, purposeful, and eternal guiding power—God—is their most beloved rock of personal peace and strength. Trust or hope in a guiding power, universal spirit, eternal source, divinity in all things, or wise and loving personal God to guide us through the joys and pains of life can add to a sense of purpose and connection to the universe and humanity. But other people who have a purely nonreligious, naturalistic view of the universe are also able to find sources of strength and peace in their lives. All of us can find strength in being part of something more—whether that more is family, friends, community, humanity, nature, causes that we highly value, or God. By taking some time to really think and feel things through, each of us can find those core big-picture perspectives that not only make sense to us but also contribute to our well-being.

My father grew up in sparse rural conditions during the Great Depression, and he worked hard to help his parents and siblings survive economically. His college education was interrupted when he enlisted in the Navy during World War II, but he finally graduated with a master's degree at the age of thirty-three. Within a short time he lost a business and a home and was in debt. He spent much of the rest of his life struggling financially to raise five children. But my father was never bitter and never complained about the bad hand that life sometimes dealt him, and through it all he found strength in his faith. In the same way that his belief in gravity served him well in the physical world, his personal religious beliefs served him well in his spiritual and ethical worlds. While the specifics of my beliefs are different from the religious tradition I was born into, I too have found peace in my big-picture belief in a guiding power in the universe.

It's a statistical reality that most people take on the worldview of the family that they are born into. According to Dr. Bernard Spilka of the University of Denver, the empirical data shows the following:

"If you had been born into a devout Muslim family, today you would probably be bowing to Mecca. If you had been raised as a Pentecostal, you would probably sometimes speak in tongues. If your parents had been confirmed atheists, you would probably not believe in God today. If you had grown up in a particular native culture, you would probably believe in many gods."

Despite this strong tendency, as with any other belief we've been given by our family or culture, we can take the time to examine our big worldviews. Do they make sense to us? And just as importantly, do they do us any good?

Whatever our specific individual beliefs about religion, spirituality, and the larger purpose of the universe, on a practical basis we are not limited in this natural world by the purposes of survival and procreation. We are gifted with the purposes that come with mind, the purposes of experiencing this world and consciously participating in a life journey. Within this innate power to experience—and within our own unique set of circumstances—life grants us the opportunity to choose a larger personal purpose:

- What we will do
- How we will live
- What we will value
- Who we will love
- What we will live for
- What we will die for

We have the opportunity to experience awe, devotion, and reverence for those things we most highly treasure; to experience wisdom and kindness, the highest expressions of mind; to experience family and friends; to alleviate pain and suffering; to endure, transform, and overcome. We are also gifted with the ability to enhance our personal well-being by adopting reasonable beliefs, choosing to do good, and letting go of the things that don't matter or that we cannot change.

SUMMARY FOR SKILL 9

Choosing Your Big Worldview: Cosmic Beliefs

As humans, we not only adopt everyday beliefs and rules about ourselves, others, and life, but we have the miraculous, innate ability to consider big-picture beliefs about the meaning and purpose of the universe and our place in it— beliefs about whether the universe is intentional or not.

Since we will never know the absolute Truth of these matters in this life, we need to accept our core assumptions about these issues with some level of faith, regardless of what those assumptions are.

As with other beliefs, we also need to consider the cash value of these cosmic beliefs.

Whether religious or not, do these beliefs prompt us to do good, treat others well, and have less internal turmoil? What are the fruits of our beliefs? Do they do us any good?

Taking the time to consider these beliefs and modifying them if they don't make sense or serve us well can be important for our well-being.

We are better off coming to terms with our beliefs and being at peace with them than being in turmoil over them or with those who believe differently than we do.

Part Two

WATER

THE PEACE OF LETTING GO

Simple Forms of Letting Go

∿

*If, in our heart, we still cling to anything—anger,
anxiety, or possessions—we cannot be free.*

THICH NHAT HANH

Mohandas Gandhi was innately shy as a young boy and avoided all company. His mind was filled with fears of ghosts, thieves, and snakes. Later he pursued a college education and adopted Western dress and customs—the latter out of fear of being looked down upon if he dressed otherwise. However, the social and political repression of his people brought him to an important personal awakening. He found that he was living a life that was not of his own choosing and filled with much fear. One by one, he let go of the shyness, anger, fears, borrowed customs, and possessions that he felt were burdening his life. In the process of letting go, he grew into the full measure of his personhood and of his contribution to his nation and the world.

Happiness is supported on the bedrock of reasonable thinking and sustained through the power of letting go. I use the metaphor of water for letting go because water is impermanent, flowing, and life-giving. Lao-Tzu also used water as a metaphor when he wrote, "The highest good is like water. Water gives life to the 10,000 things and does not strive. It flows in places that men reject."

Learning to let go can be as enlivening as the flow of a refreshing stream of water. Holding on too tightly to everyday desires, irritations, and worries can be counterproductive to well-being. Letting events drift on by when they don't matter or can't be changed—just like dropping leaves into a flowing stream—can bring greater peace of mind.

A simple form of letting go is to soften and relax what we tell ourselves in tense, frustrating moments. When we have a hunger pain, we can make it worse by holding tightly to it, which we do by telling ourselves, "I'm starving," "I've got to eat," "This is awful," or "I can't wait," and by allowing our emotions to run wild. It helps to learn to relax our thoughts and feelings about the hunger with more supportive words such as, "It's not that bad," "It won't kill me," "My feelings are making it worse than it is." When we have been offended by another person, we can hold on to our anger or hurt ("He's terrible," "I hate him," "I'll never talk to her again") or, if we truly value the relationship, we can express ourselves to the person and let go of our grudge or bitterness ("We need to talk this through," "I'll feel better if we resolve this"). We can do this with feelings and sensations in many other areas of our lives. We can let go of *everything* from time to time.

We experience letting go naturally on an ongoing basis. In one moment we might let go of a thought about going to the store and move to a thought about making a telephone call. In another, we might let go of a sensation of boredom and move to a thought of riding a bicycle. Every night we let go of one state of consciousness (being awake) and move to another (being asleep). The more we consciously apply this ability of letting go when it comes to our everyday worries, frustrations, and fears, the more of a habit it will become and the greater our peace of mind will be. This is what happened for Gandhi.

Letting go is relaxing mentally. It is usually easier to relax the physical body than it is to relax the mind. With the body, we can simply stop activity and rest. We can consciously stop our body from moving, notice each part of it, and let go of any tension until each part is fully at rest. Sometimes when we relax physically, it helps us to relax mentally. But not always. We can relax physically and still have thoughts and emotions chasing through our minds. We can be in full physical repose and still have anxiety or worries floating through our heads. In order to relax mentally we need to let go of mental turmoil, conflict, and judgment. Instead of letting go of a clenched fist, we let go of a clenched mind.

Being overly attached to things, ideas, thoughts, feelings, past events, or anything else is the reverse of letting go. Letting go means to stop grasping. There is much emphasis in Eastern thought (i.e., Hinduism, Buddhism, and Taoism) on the principle of nonattachment. This thinking maintains that the suffering in the world is due primarily to the attachment we have to our likes and dislikes. If these attachments become particularly strong, we can spend our lives in the constant search, turmoil, and struggle involved in fleeing pain and chasing pleasure. Letting go means toning down our tendency to judge, worry, fret, or envy on the basis of the push and pull of strong likes and dislikes.

Happiness studies through the years seem to confirm that even though incomes have increased dramatically since World War II, people across the globe are not a lot happier. People, especially in the developed nations, have a lot and can buy more, but they aren't necessarily satisfied. How is this possible? According to psychologists, we are only satisfied if our desires are met. With increasing incomes, however, people commonly increase their desires. When we're just starting out, we're satisfied living in a small apartment. When we have a larger income we switch our desire to having our own home. With even more money, we sometimes want a larger home, and so on. Letting go is essentially getting off this unending emotional carnival ride by reducing our desires. We can satisfy our desires by having more income, but we can also satisfy our desires by having fewer of them and being content with what we already have. The higher our expectations (desires) and the more often they are not met, the less our subjective well-being will be. As author George MacDonald wrote, "To have what we want is riches; but to be able to do without is power."

None of this means that there's something wrong with having natural likes and dislikes. It's only natural that we actively pursue our needs, wants, interests, objectives, and joys in our everyday lives. But it does mean that we need not become overly attached to them. Or as Gandhi put it, "You may have occasion to possess or use material things, but the secret of life lies in never missing them."

Letting go also means that we do not become overly attached to outcomes or need certain outcomes to be happy. We don't need to be so attached to having everything go our way that we suffer internally when it doesn't. Nonattachment means accepting the reality of life as both joy and pain, as both ease and hardship, rather than expecting life to meet the needs of our unique likes and dislikes. When the Greek philosopher Zeno (the father of the Stoic philosophical school) experienced a shipwreck that resulted in the loss of all of his possessions, his response was, "Fortune bids me to philosophize with a lighter pack."

The British actress and humanitarian Audrey Hepburn was raised in the difficult, tumultuos times of World War II. During her childhood and adolescence in German-occupied Holland she suffered from malnutrition, illness, and a lack of warm shelter, endured the separation of family members, and witnessed the tragedy of wartime violence firsthand. Perhaps as a result of her experiences she dedicated much of her time in her adult life to helping children in need, particularly through UNICEF. Her life experiences also taught her to let go of strong attachments to outcomes, to accept life for what it is. In her personal life she preferred the easy simplicity of family and country living with little fanfare. "I decided, very early on, just to accept life unconditionally," she once said. "I never expected it to do anything special for me, yet I seemed to accomplish far more than I had ever hoped."

I have to admit that while the Eastern philosophy relating to detachment makes great sense to me when it comes to things that don't matter or that we can't change, I remain quite attached to my loved ones, my core values, my special causes, and my running and hiking shoes (not to mention a fresh piece of salmon once in a while!)—and probably many more things than I'm willing to admit. I'm willing to live with the suffering that comes from time to time as a result of these and other attachments. Nonetheless, there is much to consider in this ancient, practical wisdom. We live for a relatively short time on this planet and take nothing physical with us when we leave. We're just passing through. By definition, the fewer the attachments, the greater the freedom. Why get too attached?

It can make good sense to consciously think about our attachments and consider whether we're making too big a deal out of them. We can take the following inventory from time to time:

PHYSICAL ATTACHMENTS

- "What do I *really* need in life?"
- "What do I currently have that is in excess of what I really need?"
- "Do any of these excess items cause me hassle mentally or financially? Do they get in the way of my peace of mind?"
- "What's the worst thing that could happen if I simply got rid of these excess items?"

- Or, as Marie Kondo suggests in her popular book *The Life-Changing Magic of Tidying Up,* ask the question, "Does this spark joy?" when considering any of our material goods.

MENTAL "WORRY" ATTACHMENTS

- "What do I *really* need to worry about in life?"
- "What do I currently worry about in life that I don't need to be worrying about any more?"
- "Do I like any of this excess worry? Does it do me any good?"
- "What's the worst thing that could happen if I started mentally letting go of any excess worry as I would an old pair of unneeded shoes? What kind of time limit can I give myself to worry about things?"

I once worked in a small rest home, and one of the residents, Ed, was a crusty old former construction worker who had also served in the military. Ed had become nearly crippled with severe arthritis. It was very difficult for him to get out of bed every morning, and he had every reason to complain about the suffering that life had caused him. But his common—almost daily—words of wisdom were as follows: "There are only two things to worry about: whether you're healthy or sick. If you're healthy there's nothing to worry about, and if you're sick there are only two things to worry about: whether you die or live. If you live, there's nothing to worry about, and if you die there are only two things to worry about: whether you go to heaven or hell. If you go to heaven, there's nothing to worry about, and if you go to hell, you'll be shaking hands with so many buddies that you'll soon forget that there was anything to worry about!"

SUMMARY FOR SKILL 10

Simple Forms of Letting Go

Letting go of things we can't change or that don't really matter is an important skill to develop in order to enhance well-being.

Two simple forms of letting go are:

(1) to soften and relax what we tell ourselves in tense, frustrating moments, and

(2) to reduce the amount of things to which we have strong attachments (both physical and mental) and, in particular, to let go of attachments to the outcomes in our lives over which we have little control.

Nonjudgmental Awareness in Everyday Living

~~

To be awake is to be alive.

HENRY DAVID THOREAU

My father had a humorous habit of being so absorbed in thought that he was unaware of things around him. He was a high school teacher and regardless of whether he was at school or driving his car down the main street of our small town, he would never see us when we waved to him. When he was at home, he could get so absorbed in crossword puzzles that he wouldn't hear a word we said if we tried to have a conversation. I used to make fun of this—along with his loud snoring—but as life would have it, I turned out to have both habits. I have been known to drive by major fires, accidents, friends, and family without ever seeing them, and I can get so absorbed in books that I don't hear a thing that others are saying to me.

It's fine to get absorbed in interesting things, but if we don't listen to people, they may stop talking to us. If we don't pay attention to our loved ones, people in need, our values, our behavior, and our inner lives, we may miss out on some of the most important features of our life experience.

Letting go first requires becoming *aware* of what is going on. Awareness is our innate ability to notice and observe. With our awareness, we're able to more fully experience both the outer world and our inner world through our "mind's eye." Enhancing our inner lives requires us to apply this conscious awareness. If we want to counter unreasonable thinking, we first need to pay attention to the thoughts and emotions flowing through us. In order to transform harmful behavior, we first need to be aware of how we're behaving. In order to live a full life, we need to be totally aware of what we value most and live in harmony with those values. And in order to let go, we need to first see what we're holding on to.

Becoming aware can be a life-changing awakening. By the age of thirty, Millard Fuller was a millionaire with luxury cars, speed boats, lots of real estate, and everything else that money could buy. But he was also on the verge of divorce and losing his family and his health. He awakened to the fact that building his business was costing him everything that he truly cared about. He found that he was living a life that actually devalued what he valued most. This awakening led Millard and his wife, Linda, to sell everything and give much of the proceeds to churches, colleges, and charities. They then began to build houses for people in need in southern Georgia. Millard and Linda Fuller went on to found Habitat for Humanity, an organization that helps people in need throughout the world. Becoming aware changed not only the lives of the Fullers but also the lives of people without shelter around the world.

Beyond the big changes that awareness can produce, the practice of greater awareness on a personal, everyday basis allows us to live our lives more fully and helps us in letting go. Zen masters train their students to cultivate a special type of awareness called mindfulness. Mindfulness is nonjudgmentally paying attention in the present moment on purpose. It includes focusing, monitoring, and accepting. Mindfulness can be applied to every aspect of our everyday lives: our work, our relationships, and our inner life. To help develop mindfulness, serious practitioners engage in meditation wherein they use a special focus of attention: their own breath, a special word, their natural surroundings, yoga movements, walking, or other objects of attention. If the mind strays from the focus of concentration, the practitioner also pays attention to that straying and then gently lets go of it and returns to the original focus of concentration. This training in and of itself can help a person develop the ability to let go.

As a general principle of well-being, mindfulness can help us more fully experience the moments of our lives. For example, mindfulness means that when we eat, we truly experience and enjoy our meal. We notice the details in the flavor and scent of the food. We savor it.

When we are talking to people, mindfulness means that we are truly present in the conversation. We fully listen and seek to understand. Rather than immediately focusing on *judging* what the person is telling us, we first focus on *understanding* what the person is saying and trying to comprehend his or her perspective. We let go of distractions and focus on the conversation. Once we have taken the mindful step of striving to understand what the person is saying and feeling, we can respond more thoughtfully.

Mindfulness can also play an important role in helping us change our relationship to unpleasant feelings that flow through us. Rather than focusing on what we don't like about a feeling, with mindfulness we simply sit with that feeling and let it happen. By simply being with and monitoring what's happening inside, we can help settle the "mud" that tumultuous feelings can sometimes stir up in the streams of our inner life. Without judgment, what does the feeling actually feel like?

Sometimes mindfulness teachers metaphorically compare this nonjudgmental awareness of our inner world to how we might interact with a waterfall. We can stand in the middle of the waterfall of our thoughts and feelings, or we can step aside and learn to watch this waterfall without struggling to stop it or run away from it. This does not naively mean that we do not still feel the impact of unpleasant emotions, only that we see them for what they are and take them less personally.

In his book *In My Own Words*, the Dalai Lama suggested that one of the best places to begin the cultivation of an "awakening mind" is to get in the habit of noticing the feelings we have toward other people: friends, strangers, and enemies (if we have any). If we can begin to notice and let go of feelings of dislike and anger toward people, we not only fill our own hearts with happier emotions but we help to make the world better for those around us. He also maintained that any form of mindful awareness does not come through intellectual understanding or wishful thinking but only through practice.

By really trying to notice and let go of the natural judgment and related tumult that sometimes comes to us in human relationships and greater striving to understand people—their nature and their suffering—rather than focusing so strongly on ourselves, we begin to develop more compassion. Although as a monk the Dalai Lama is in the practice of meditation, study, and prayer for five and a half hours every day (he rises at 3:30 a.m. each morning!), it is interesting to note that for him the most awakened mind is the one filled with compassion for others. He humbly acknowledges that he does not yet fully have this "awakening mind" but believes strongly that it is one of the greatest benefits of nonjudgmental awareness.

There are many simple ways to experiment with and experience nonjudgmental awareness (mindfulness) in our everyday lives. Here are some suggestions:

- Sit for a few minutes each day, just paying attention to your breathing and letting go of everything else. When you breathe in, your stomach goes out like a balloon filling with air; when you breathe out, it should go in like a balloon deflating. This can be like your own portable version of sitting by the sea. When you pay attention, breathing in can sound like waves coming in to shore, and breathing out, like waves going back out to sea. As your mind drifts, just return to paying attention to the breath.

- You can pay more attention to and savor the sensations of everyday mundane activities. When you shower, fully enjoy the water. When you prepare or eat food, really notice the ingredients, tastes, and aromas. When you do yard work, experience the soil, plants, water, and sunshine. When you shop, slow down and take in the active sights and sounds.

- When you walk outdoors, whether to get some place or for a leisurely stroll, you can take in the full experience and sensation of bodily movement and enjoy your surroundings. You can let go of daily worries that creep in and completely accept the world as it is in that moment.

- In your interaction with other people, you can slow down and give them your full attention. No need to answer your cell phone, multitask, or rush to give an opinion; you can take the opportunity to just fully listen.

- In relating with those especially close to you, you can give them more of your nonjudgmental compassion. Everyone needs someone who can provide them with acceptance and understanding. You can be that person for your loved ones.

- If you have stressful thoughts and feelings whirling around in your mind, you can stop and nonjudgmentally observe them for what they are, accepting them as part of your imperfect human body and experience. If the content of your thoughts can be changed to make them more reasonable, change them. If not, just accept the tumult as you would a waterfall, until it's run its course.

SUMMARY FOR SKILL 11

Nonjudgmental Awareness in Everyday Living

One of the key skills required in letting go is the ability to use our awareness to observe what's going on, without judgment and without overreaction.

Just the very act of observing life with less judgment is an act of letting go (the act of letting go of the mental turmoil that often comes with judgment).

Mindfulness meditation practitioners develop this skill formally by taking the time to sit and pay attention to their breath or other object, and letting go of distractions and judgments.

Any of us can practice this skill in our everyday lives. We can choose to pay more attention, with less judgment, to the people in our lives, our work tasks, our moments of fun, and our general surroundings.

We can also practice simply observing the unpleasant thoughts and feelings that flow through our minds with less judgment, rather than fighting them or struggling with them and thus increasing their impact.

Acceptance as a Portal to Letting Go

~~~

Acceptance doesn't mean resignation; it means understanding that something is what it is.

MICHAEL J. FOX

One hot summer day my father, brothers, brother-in-law, nephews, and I hiked into the Sierras for a greatly anticipated day of trout fishing. Fortunately for the fish, we didn't have much luck. On the other hand, the water was great. We came across a pristine pool of deep, clear water and spent much of the afternoon diving and swimming. As outdoors people know, there is nothing quite as refreshing as diving off a rock into a deep pool of cold water on a hot day. In those moments, the body is one with nature and all the cares of the world are lost. Everything becomes quite simple.

Acceptance is like this. Acceptance is jumping off the rocky cliff of mental and emotional turmoil into the clear, deep pool of nonjudgment and nonattachment. Acceptance is letting go in action. Too often in everyday living, we struggle in the "heat" of things that don't matter, when we could be swimming around in the clear, cool waters of acceptance.

Some things really matter in life: meeting our physical needs, good relationships with those close to us, healthy core beliefs, family and civic responsibilities, and personal causes and interests. Fortunately, many of these things are also things that we can do something about.

But there are many everyday irritations, worries, and disagreements that really don't matter. In the scheme of things, whether someone cuts us off in traffic, whether we forget something on our shopping list, whether my spouse wants to watch a different television program than me, whether the weather is cold, or whether my favorite football team wins, just doesn't matter. In the hustle and bustle of everyday life and the nitty-gritty of personal relationships, one of the most powerful reminders we can give ourselves is that it just doesn't matter, when it really doesn't.

Likewise, if there are everyday issues that we either have no choice over or no ability or intention of doing anything about, there is no benefit to churning over them. It's human nature to banter with ourselves and others over topics like people, politics, religion, and sports, and sometimes it can be fun. But sometimes it's not fun and can add more stress to our lives than we want. On those occasions when we prefer peace, it can again help to remind ourselves that it just doesn't matter.

In the film *Meatballs*, Bill Murray plays a camp counselor working for a cut-rate summer camp called North Star. The camp's nemesis is the much more wealthy, athletic Mohawk camp across the lake. The Mohawks have beaten the North Star campers in their annual Olympiad for twelve straight years. When the North Star camp is feeling the gloom of the impending annual event, Murray rouses the camp with his motivational "It just doesn't matter" speech. In stirring words he reminds everyone of the obvious: it really doesn't matter to the lives of the North Star kids if they win a camp contest. A collective light bulb goes off in the minds of the camp kids and soon they are whooping and hollering to the energetic chant of "It just doesn't matter." Sometimes without thinking, we get so quickly and automatically invested in the emotional turmoil of events that we skip the really big step of asking ourselves the obvious: does this really matter to us—and if so why? My kind New England mother-in-law was fond of phrasing this differently, "In fifty years this won't matter." This has always stuck with me and is surely true of many of our everyday worries and cares. If something will matter in fifty years, then maybe it's worth taking seriously; if not, then maybe not so much.

On the other hand, some of the things that really do matter to us in life can also be sources of great pain. Some losses, mistakes, and accidents are catastrophic and unalterable. Illness, poverty, and the deaths of loved ones can all be sources of immense suffering. In these cases, saying, "It just doesn't matter" is both untrue and hollow. But it *is* completely true that these experiences are a built-in part of this difficult life and finding even a measure of peace in the midst of great suffering requires finally accepting this truth. Sometimes we have to accept pain (including emotional pain) before it will lessen. Grieving is the process of accepting difficult losses. As William James once wrote, "Acceptance of what has happened is the first step to overcoming the consequences of any misfortune." We can wish that the world were free of losses, mistakes, and accidents, but it's not. We can wish that we were perfect, but we aren't. We can wish we would not experience pain and suffering, but we do. We are in denial of the world we are born into to think otherwise. *We are imperfect people living in an imperfect world.*

C. S. Lewis was an author, literary critic, and professor at both Oxford and Cambridge Universities in England during the 1920s to 1960s. He was raised in Belfast, Northern Ireland, and after arriving at Oxford for his college education, he volunteered as a soldier in World War I, during which he was wounded in trench warfare. He had become an atheist as a teenager, but while teaching at Oxford, he became friends with J.R.R. Tolkien (the author of *The Lord of the Rings*), who helped to convert Lewis to Christianity.

Lewis thereafter became a writer on popular themes about Christianity. But following the death of his American wife, Joy, after just three years of marriage, Lewis went through a period of great despair and grief. As documented in his book *A Grief Observed*, nothing provided him with much relief, including his religious beliefs. He writes in his book:

> "For in grief nothing 'stays put.' One keeps on emerging from a phase, but it always recurs. ... How often—will it be for always?—how often will the vast emptiness astonish me like a complete novelty and make me say, "I never realized my loss till this moment"? The same leg is cut off time after time."

His book is a poignant, searing meditation on the extreme difficulty of losing a loved one, and in the end he concludes, "Aren't all these notes the senseless writings of a man who won't accept the fact that there is nothing we can do with suffering except to suffer it?" We can and should seek out help when we're suffering, but in the end, there is no way to deal with some levels of suffering over things that we cannot change except to accept the suffering.

Acceptance is the primary portal to letting go. We usually can't let go by just telling ourselves to do so. We need to go through the mental shift of accepting the event or emotion that is causing us turmoil. Acceptance means stopping the resistance and avoidance and simply letting things be as they are. It means being willing, open, and receptive to experiencing events no matter how painful. When we accept, we stop judging. We stop telling ourselves what we don't like about something that is difficult or unpleasant for us. We simply experience it. It doesn't mean that we have to forget— as if we could. But if we cannot change difficulties, we simply let them be. Acceptance does not mean evaluating things positively or having to like them; it means seeing reality as it is with less mental struggle or emotional turmoil. Michael J. Fox, who has endured several years of living with Parkinson's disease, once shared the following quote in *AARP* magazine, "My happiness goes in direct proportion to my acceptance, and in inverse proportion to my expectations."

Acceptance also does not mean that we still don't try to make things better, including dealing with the irritations of everyday life. Even as we accept and stop churning internally about the weather and bad traffic, we can still make things more pleasant by having a cold drink or turning on the radio—the idea is not to become an ascetic monk but to reduce internal stress and turmoil.

Acceptance is enhanced by making sure that we have reasonable core beliefs about ourselves, others, and life. If we don't begin with a core acceptance that life is imperfect, filled with both good and bad, we will live a life of continual turmoil and frustration. Our expectations will not be in synch with how life really is. If we expect ourselves and others to be consistently perfect, we will be filled with anger and disappointment as everyday imperfections naturally unfold in the actual world we live in. In order to learn to accept difficult, unalterable events, big and small, it helps to first accept life. William James wrote in the *Varieties of Religious Experience*: "At bottom the whole concern of both morality and religion is with the manner of our acceptance of the universe. Do we accept it only in part and grudgingly, or heartily and altogether?"

Acceptance is also greatly enhanced by applying mindfulness: to practice just noticing events (both internal and external ones) without judging them. Rather than avoiding and running away from unpleasantness, we directly acknowledge it. By not judging, we can more clearly see events with greater understanding. We're not so focused on changing things, as we are on letting them be. Some things are worth fighting for in life, but many issues and events aren't worth fighting for at all. Simply paying attention and seeking understanding will help us discover which is which.

"Radical acceptance" is a leap beyond acceptance as an occasional coping tool. Radical acceptance is incorporating into one's everyday living a fundamental attitude of acceptance of everything. It means opening up fully to "what is" and relaxing judgment or defensive mechanisms. It means complete acceptance of self, our emotions, others, and the world in this very moment, in spite of flaws and imperfections. It doesn't mean being passive or evaluating everything positively or accepting harmful and destructive behavior without response. It means seeing things more directly as they are, not as we want them to be, with the understanding that in some matters we have the power of choice and in some matters we don't. Arthur Rubinstein once wrote, "Of course there is no formula for success except, perhaps, an unconditional acceptance of life and what it brings."

I know from personal experience that radical acceptance is difficult to maintain, but even moments of radical acceptance can bring greater peace and insight.

Consider practicing acceptance in the following ways:

- When we are worrying, a big question to keep asking ourselves is whether we are worrying about something that we can actually do anything about. The low-hanging fruit of acceptance is to start with the things we have no power to change. There is absolutely no value in spending our emotional cash on problems we cannot solve.

- When feeling everyday emotional turmoil, don't skip the step of asking yourself if the situation that is causing the turmoil really matters. If not, consciously remind yourself that it just doesn't matter.

- The next time you're in a traffic jam or in a long line, practice accepting the situation for what it is rather than letting frustration and turmoil have its way. A traffic jam is a natural part of life—too many cars in one place—and there's nothing to be done about it. You don't have to love it, but you also don't need to battle it emotionally because it will not do any good (and may actually do your body harm).

- When you find yourself in a conflict with one of your children or your spouse, sometimes it's good to stop and ask yourself if the battle is worth fighting. Does any of this really matter? And if so, why? Sometimes battles are important to wage because something significant is at stake, but too often conflict is just a bad habit driven by our imperfect, noisy emotions.

- If we are struggling with deep suffering over losses that we cannot change, in addition to getting help from others, our only other way through may be acceptance—being willing to let sorrow and grief happen rather than fight them.

- Try moments of complete, unconditional "radical acceptance," moments when you accept everything in the world in that point in time as "It is what it is."

SUMMARY FOR SKILL 12

Acceptance as a Portal to Letting Go

It's not always easy to let go just by telling ourselves to do so. Acceptance is the primary portal to letting go.

We practice acceptance by going through the mental shift of accepting the event or emotion that is causing us turmoil.

Acceptance means stopping mental struggle, resistance, and avoidance and simply letting things be as they are. It means being willing, open, and receptive to experience events even though they are painful.

Acceptance does not mean evaluating things positively or having to like them. With constructive acceptance we still change what we can, but with a clear-eyed view of how things are and with less inner tumult.

For things that really aren't that important, we can remind ourselves that it just doesn't matter. But for serious events that we cannot change, in addition to getting the help that we can, we accept both the events and the suffering that comes with them.

Acceptance as a Tool for Dealing with Unpleasant Emotions

~~~

I have accepted fear as part of life—specifically the
fear of change . . . I have gone ahead despite the
pounding in the heart that says turn back.

ERICA JONG

I have not known anyone in this life who has perfect emotions—who feels worry or guilt only when they need to. The
longer I live, the more clear it becomes that part of living in
an imperfect world is to experience natural emotions that are
also imperfect—sometimes heartbreakingly so. One morning
my good friend Dave, an earthly "saint" in my book, sat up
in his bed after his loved ones had left for the day, picked up
a gun, and killed himself. He was in the prime of his life and
had everything to live for, but he was afflicted with a seriously
imperfect emotional makeup, not of his own choosing. In the
end, these imperfect emotions were too much for him to bear.
We do not choose these painful emotions that naturally flow
through us, and dealing with them can be the most difficult
human challenge of all.

In the allegorical story of Adam and Eve in the Bible, Adam and Eve are innocent until they eat the fruit of the "tree of knowledge of good and evil." Once they have this ability to know and experience good and evil, their simple lives are changed forever. With this new knowledge, they are forced to leave their paradise of innocence (the Garden of Eden) and enter the world of human awareness, emotion, and suffering. Other creatures of the animal kingdom are left in this state of innocence, but humans are not. The possibility of evil and suffering is the price paid for having advanced human consciousness. Suffering is not abnormal in our human world—it's a natural part of the human condition.

Transforming our thinking habits and beliefs can benefit our emotional lives. Solving personal problems can help reduce unhappiness. But nothing can change the fact that we live in a natural world of both joy and pain, including natural emotional pain. In the same way our bodies can be generally healthy but still experience physical pain that is unique to our specific body, so too can we experience emotional pain that is unique to each of us. Our inner lives are affected by our inborn humanity and by our innate negativity bias, not just by how we consciously think or behave.

In a perfect world, we would only feel fear or anger when something was truly dangerous. We would only feel worry when we needed to prepare for a possible life-threatening event. But in the imperfect world we actually live in, depending upon our DNA and other factors, we can have these unpleasant feelings much more than we need to. As Daniel Goleman points out in *Emotional Intelligence*, from the time we're toddlers, each of us can have a very different emotional thermostat. Some of us are born with a quicker temper, more fear, extra worry, bouts of panic, or too much or too little guilt. Children and adults alike can by nature be more prone to anxiety, sadness, and depression. Changing thoughts doesn't always change emotional pain any more than changing thoughts can easily change physical pain. In fact, our emotions can overwhelm reasoning to the point at which our emotions become our truth, no matter how flawed.

When our daughter, Brooke, was three years old, she had a natural fear of dogs. We didn't realize this until we actually brought home our dog Ozzie as a puppy. Brooke obviously didn't choose or want this fear, but she couldn't be around this strange, fuzzy, little creature without crying and wanting to be on a chair or table so that the dog couldn't touch her. Miraculously, just as we were considering giving away the dog, Brooke began to warm to him. She had apparently been around him enough to become less sensitive to him. We had her hold his leash, and she felt less vulnerable. She was soon hugging and playing with him.

An additional point that Goleman makes is that we can modify natural tendencies that don't serve us well. A naturally shy person can become less shy by jumping in and meeting new people. A natural worrier can worry less by becoming more solution oriented and changing thinking habits (realizing when it just doesn't matter). A naturally angry person can become less volatile by learning to walk away from aggressive situations. We can make conscious efforts to modify natural habits of thinking and behavior that are counter productive. And while certain emotional tendencies may be innate, we need to take responsibility for our behavior, including making up for harm that is emotionally driven. A quick temper or too little guilt cannot be an excuse for harmful behavior.

But even after all we've reasonably done, we will still experience natural emotional discomfort and suffering in our lives that is unique to each of us. Rather than adding to our pain through the greater mental struggle and turmoil that comes with nonacceptance, we can lessen the pain through *acceptance*. When we strive to change unreasonable thinking, we work to change the *content* of our internal events. However, with acceptance, we work to modify our *relationship* with these events. We are open to and accepting of them rather than bent on avoiding them. Just as we accept some of the natural aches and pains of our physical body, we begin to view our innate, difficult-to-change emotions as part of life rather than as problems to be solved. Unpleasant emotions that do not benefit us are akin to "emotional noise" that is neither useful nor pleasant, but can be accepted and lived with.

In the world of professional psychology, exposure-based procedures have become helpful tools in the treatment of emotional anxiety. People are often able to become less fearful of snakes, heights, social events, and other personally difficult situations by being exposed to them gradually and in various ways (in photographs, in imagination, and in actual reality). This also applies to thoughts and emotions themselves. As a Zen master once said, "We can invite our fear to tea." By monitoring our natural, unpleasant emotions rather than trying to escape them, and simply letting them happen without dread or struggle, we can begin to change our relationship to those emotions. They may still be uncomfortable, but we are less sensitive to them.

I'm not an expert on depression, but I had a brief episode of depression following the death of our beautiful fourteen-year old niece Katie several years ago. It was the first time I had experienced the death of a much-too-young loved one (I later experienced the deeply sorrowful loss of our nephew Doug, who was a much-too-young father). When Katie was killed in a car accident, I experienced a grief I had never felt before. I felt sorrow for my brother and his family and for the enormous loss her death meant for all of us. I could not sleep, eat, or find solace. I would not dare to compare my experience to the grief of my brother and his family, but I do know that no measure of reasoning or talking back to my sorrowful thoughts had any effect. After a few days, this grief for others slipped into concern for me. I started to worry about whether I would ever be able to pull out of the darkness.

As C. S. Lewis expressed so well in *A Grief Observed:*

"Part of every misery is, so to speak, the misery's shadow or reflection: the fact that you don't merely suffer but have to keep on thinking about the fact that you suffer. I not only live each endless day in grief, but live each day thinking about living each day in grief."

I felt this enough to know something of what he was talking about, and this prompted me to seek advice from my wife, Julie, who *is* an expert on pain. Since young adulthood, Julie has struggled with the *daily* physical pain of rheumatoid arthritis. I asked her how one copes with pain that does not go away. She taught me that at some point I needed to accept the pain itself. Mentally fighting or denying emotional pain that will not go away only worsens the pain and makes it more difficult to function. She explained that an emotional wound is no less real than a physical wound. It does little good to hate or wish away wounds that have not healed and may never completely heal ("amputations," as C. S. Lewis called them); this only creates greater pain. By accepting our pain, and acknowledging it for what it is, we can let go of the additional inner turmoil. Or as Julie would say—in contradiction to purist Zen thinking—once we accept our unpleasant pain, we can then better ignore it and go about living our lives the best we can.

Julie's advice on accepting pain was invaluable, and it turns out to be consistent with the thinking and clinical experience of specialists in acceptance therapy. Acceptance therapy, formally called acceptance and commitment therapy (ACT), is based on the principle of noticing and accepting our internal mental events—especially difficult and unwanted ones—rather than hating them or trying to get rid of them. ACT was developed in the 1980s through the work of Steven Hayes of the University of Nevada, Reno, and others. It was developed as another tool to help people with emotional difficulty for whom cognitive-behavioral tools or medicine were not fully sufficient. A few core principles of ACT include the following:

- Practicing the skill of monitoring our natural feelings from a third-party-observer point of view
- Viewing unhelpful thoughts and emotions as sensations or mental "objects" rather than latching on to them or overidentifying with their content
- Mindfully accepting unpleasant, difficult-to-change thoughts and emotions by observing them and letting them come and go without worrying about them or struggling to escape from them—and without judging them
- Keeping a focus on our own values and living an actively engaged life based on those values, regardless of our unpleasant emotions.

According to ACT theory and practice, treating unpleasant thoughts and feelings as just thoughts and feelings (rather than as "self") can help reduce the threat of those thoughts and feelings and the anxiety involved in trying to avoid and eliminate them. ACT is also based on coming in more direct contact with the part of us that simply observes and experiences. This is our "transcendent" self. It's the part of self that is consciously aware of everything else, including our thoughts and feelings; the part of self that has the ability to more objectively gain perspective. The goal of the ACT approach isn't so much to alleviate emotional discomfort as it is to help people accept and live with emotional discomfort if necessary, so that they can get on with the rest of their lives.

Physical events themselves are not what disturb our inner world; it's the emotions that accompany them. As the Greek philosopher Epictetus maintained, "For it is not death or pain that is to be feared, but the fear of death or pain." Our emotions can make us not only fearful of physical events but also of mental events. Specialists maintain that anxiety disorders intensify when people struggle to avoid the experience of anxiety. Fretting over anxious emotions can make that anxiety even worse.

Acceptance of unpleasant emotions does not mean that we judge them positively, only that rather than trying to avoid or escape them, we open ourselves to contact with them and let them jump all around as they may. Accepting a painful emotion means to simply let it happen, without fight or anguish and especially without judgment of ourselves. We accept these emotions as part of the imperfect world we live in.

In one very dramatic case, the comedian Maria Bamford told of how she had suffered well into her thirties from seriously obsessive thoughts of worry and anxiety. As an example, she would have obsessive thoughts about doing something violent to people close to her, and her anxiety wasn't that she would actually carry out acts of violence, it was about having the thoughts themselves and what they said about her as a person, "What kind of 'bad' person would have such thoughts?" The more she tried to push them away, the more she would have them. In her case, it was only through very direct exposure/acceptance ("flooding") of her troublesome thoughts through the help of a medical specialist that she found structural relief from her decades-long malady. She is now not only able to talk about this suffering, but to do so with edgy comedy. We may not need this flooding level of exposure to obtain the benefit of acceptance, but we can all gain from greater acceptance of difficult mental events that are hard to change.

When we have an unnecessary, unpleasant emotion that our thinking or behavior can't easily alter, or that we simply don't have the energy to deal with, we can choose to consciously accept the feeling. We can tell ourselves in that moment that we're experiencing a natural unpleasant emotion. We can consciously remind ourselves that these emotions are part of life. (But twists, described on pages 87–88, can be applied not only to external events but also to internal emotional events.) To help us relate to a painful feeling as a feeling (and not as self), we can focus on understanding the nature of the pain. What is the exact sensation? What is the exact intensity? If it's overwhelming and disabling, we can treat it truly as a pain by seeking out professional medical help and the relief of medicine, just as with a physical pain.

I've been running most of my life: competitively when I was young, and *very* noncompetitively throughout much of my adult life. Even when I've been in good shape, at some point during a run I feel some level of natural emotional discomfort. It's emotional fear of pain, even though as I scan my body I don't really have much actual physical pain. It does little good to tell myself that my slow run is not a mortal threat and therefore there's no need to feel fear or emotional discomfort. I already know this, and yet I still feel discomfort. But what *has* helped me is ultimately accepting this emotion as a natural phenomenon. I don't fight it, get anxious over it, or take it personally. I see it for what it truly is—a natural emotion—and when I don't fuss over it, my run is more satisfying, even though I still experience the unpleasant emotion!

Acceptance of difficult emotions is not resignation. It's more clearly seeing and relating to our emotions for what they are: natural inner sensations that may or may not be constructive. There is no resignation in accepting physical pain after we have done what we can to alleviate such pain. Likewise, acceptance of difficult-to-change emotions is not resignation but a reasonable choice not to be limited by those emotions as we pursue the interests of our lives. In both cases, our conscious acceptance can and should include seeking out the professional medical help that we need.

According to specialists in acceptance, we can practice noticing and accepting unpleasant emotions in a variety of ways:

- As with any mindfulness exercise, we can simply sit and monitor our natural feelings, without judgment—especially when they're bothersome. We can do this by seeing our emotions for what they are and not fretting over them, being willing to be with them rather than avoiding them, and viewing them from a strictly third-party-observer perspective.

- We can experiment with noticing the distinct qualities of the sensations themselves without criticism and paying attention without worry (or paying attention to the sensation of our worries). Is it a big pain or a small? Dull or sharp? Chaotic or continuous? Is the pain to the point where we need professional medical help and the relief of medicine?

- We can practice seeing our thoughts as sensations, or "objects" rather than concrete reality. Sometimes thoughts are helpful and true, and sometimes they are unhelpful and false. In particular, overidentifying or "fusing" with thoughts to the point where we think the thoughts passing through us *are* us can cause problems.

- If you can, take a few minutes right now to observe the natural emotions that come to you when you sit in silence. I have found in doing so that my natural emotions are much more jumpy and discontented than I would have thought. They can move from contentment to anticipatory worry, anxiousness, or boredom very quickly. We can all benefit from greater nonjudgmental awareness and acceptance of our natural emotions.

SUMMARY FOR SKILL 13

Acceptance as a Tool for Dealing with Unpleasant Emotions

Some of the unpleasant feelings we experience in our lives simply come to us as part of our imperfect makeup.

By virtue of being human we all experience some level of suffering. Some level of emotional discomfort and suffering is a basic part of the human condition—it's not an abnormal exception.

In the same way that we are benefited by accepting events in our lives that we can't change, we are benefited by learning to accept natural emotions that are difficult to change.

Changing unreasonable thinking habits and beliefs as well as getting medical help for chronic emotional pain can be helpful, but we are still destined to experience some level of emotional suffering regardless of these efforts. Our well-being is enhanced by accepting, rather than fighting and avoiding, these unpleasant mental events.

We can still pursue our values and live full lives in spite of emotional discomfort by mindfully monitoring and accepting our difficult thoughts and emotions without judgment.

SKILL 14

Letting Go of Things That Don't Have Value (Integrity)

~~~

*Authentic values are those
by which a life can be lived.*

ALLAN BLOOM

Socrates was completely correct when he taught that a big part of well-being is connected to knowing ourselves. A critical part of knowing who we are is making sure we know what we value. Behaviorists have made the obvious point that our well-being can be enhanced by simply doing fewer of the things that we don't value and more of the things that we do value. That seems pretty simple, but we get so caught up in the whirlwind of the society and life that we've been born into that sometimes we don't stop to actually consider and choose our own values. Integrity is choosing to live a life in synch with what we value most.

John Muir was eleven years old in 1849 when he and his family (which included eight children) emigrated from Scotland to the United States. When he was twenty-two he enrolled in the University of Wisconsin, paid his own way through most of college, but never graduated. He had many interests, especially in the sciences, and was known for his inventiveness—particularly in working with machines. At age twenty-nine, while working in a wagon-wheel factory, an accident changed his life. A tool struck him in the eye, and for six weeks he remained in a darkened room worried about whether he would ever regain his sight. When he did regain his sight, he looked at life with new purpose. He decided that he would focus his full attention on what he valued most—the natural world. Muir simplified his life and began his lifelong quest as a champion and activist for the preservation of nature. While later in life he found a way to successfully provide for his family (and proved to be a skilled farmer and businessman), he let go of many other activities that were not of value to him. He published more than 300 articles and twelve books, was an outspoken preservationist, and cofounded the Sierra Club—becoming the "patron saint of the American wilderness." Muir influenced generations of Americans to establish national parks and to take greater care of the natural world.

Like Muir, we too can learn to let go of activities that add little cash value to our lives and to more fully engage in those activities that are consistent with our personal values. "Right effort" is most effective when focused on "right aim." We are born with fundamental physical purposes (survival and procreation), but our minds, by providing us with the ability to experience, open the door to many other possibilities, some of which we can choose for ourselves. We have many life domains that call out for us to determine our personal purpose: how we will make an income, how we will use our time and talents, how we will pursue the things we naturally enjoy, and what we will believe. For our personal well-being it makes good sense to determine our values and, as long as they are not harmful to ourselves or others, to live in congruence with them. Every so often we might reflect on our highest values and consider whether we need to tweak our lives to more fully engage them. Whether those values include family, friends, career, hobbies, or heartfelt causes, do we want to drop activities of lesser value in order to make more room for what we care about most? Even if on a practical basis we can't make major changes in our lives, can we carve out more value-added moments? When Teddy Roosevelt found himself in too many meetings that took him away from his family, he started to set up alternative "appointments" to skip out and see his children. If we love sports or art, even if we can't make a living at such endeavors, can we find more small pockets of time for them?

Choosing and living our values can simplify our lives. They can be our personal "lighthouses," helping to keep us heading in the right direction and avoiding activities that don't really have value to us. Depending upon who we are, we might actually have a number of things we value—in which case we need to prioritize our values. We can do this by taking the time to list them out and assess them using the tools suggested in the previous chapter on Solution Thinking (beginning on page 71).

Sometimes we are handed down values that we have not consciously chosen—they are given to us by our family or culture. We might be living by automatic rules about what we "should" value rather than what we really choose for ourselves. Our parents may want us to be doctors and lawyers when we want to be teachers and musicians (or vice versa). They may pass on to us certain political, religious, and cultural beliefs that we don't agree with. Our culture may want us to wear certain clothes and have a certain lifestyle when we have distaste for both. We may feel pressured to either get married when we're a certain age or to wait to get married until we are older. We may have automatically assumed from our culture of affluence that spending our lives earning more and that greater income is valuable without having ever decided if this is true for us. We may be involved in blind ambition based on someone else's values, unless we actually stop to think about them and choose for ourselves.

As documented in the book *Unstoppable* by Cynthia Kersey, Robyn Allan had been taught by her parents from an early age that "if you can't be excellent at something, don't do it." Her passion was dancing, but since she wasn't ever going to achieve greatness at it, she stopped doing it. She went on to get a master's degree in economics and became successful in a business career, but her unfulfilled passion for dance remained. At age thirty-two she decided to carve out time in her life for one of the things she had always valued most. Rather than continue to work late at the office, she left at the end of the workday and took up the dance lessons she had dropped when she was younger. Eventually she would produce, choreograph, and perform in four dance shows that played to large audiences in her home country of Canada. She would also go on to become the CEO of the Insurance Company of British Columbia, the largest insurance company in Canada. By making the commitment to herself, she discovered that she could make room for both her work and the dancing she loved.

The *commitment* part of ACT has to do with identifying what we most value and committing ourselves to those values in order to live our lives fully, despite emotions or circumstances. Kelly Wilson, a professor at the University of Mississippi and a co-developer of ACT, has identified the ten following value domains to help people determine what values are most important to them and whether they are living their lives based on those values:

1. Family relations
2. Marriage/couple relations
3. Parenting
4. Friendship/social life
5. Work/career
6. Education/personal growth

7. Recreation
8. Spirituality
9. Citizenship/community
10. Health/physical well-being

What do we truly care about? What core moral and ethical principles are absolutely not negotiable for us? What brings us joy? What brings us satisfaction? What do we really want to do? If we value ethics, friends, family, income, education, unique personal interests and talents, or something else entirely, it makes sense to live our values. This means doing more of the things that are truly important to us and less of the things that we do not value—letting go of unproductive activities that can lead us far astray.

When we examine our values, Wilson suggests asking ourselves, "In a world where you could choose to have your life be about something, what would I choose?" Another exercise is to imagine that we have died and, looking around at those who are left behind, ask ourselves, "What would I want to be remembered for?" The earlier we examine and choose our values the better; but it is never too late to refine them and to more fully live them.

Socrates lived at a time when there was great wealth in Greece, and he was greatly concerned that culturally his people had made material well-being their dominant value, without giving it much thought. When he was put on trial by his fellow citizens, who had grown weary of his challenging their money-focused culture, he said:

"I tried to persuade each of you to care first not about any of his possessions, but about himself and how he'll become best and wisest; and not primarily about the city's possessions, but about the city itself; and to care about all other things in the same way."

Authentic values are not feelings, they are actions. If we don't feel like living our truly authentic values, we live them anyway. We shut our eyes, jump into the cold pool of action, and start swimming. A life that spends too much time on things we don't value can become a life half-lived.

There is much we can do to let go of things we don't really value:

- Take the time to explore what we do value, perhaps by using the list of value domains above or simply by asking ourselves what is really important to us, what we stand for, and what we would want to be known or remembered for.

- Review our daily activities and the amount of time we spend on things we value, as opposed to the time we spend on things that don't support what we value.

- Consider any "big moves" (new careers, new civic efforts, reenergized relationships) we need to make to more fully live our values. Consider small, everyday changes (inserting pockets of activities into our daily lives) that allow us to more fully engage in and enjoy our values.

- Make choices on a daily basis that make our values a priority. Let go of other activities that get in the way of our values.

SUMMARY FOR SKILL 14

Letting Go of Things That Don't Have Value (Integrity)

Behaviorists have made the obvious point that our well-being can be enhanced by simply doing fewer of the things that we don't value and more of the things that we do value.

To do this, we first need to take the time to really explore what we value most: family, friends, ethical values, personal causes, passions, and sources of enjoyment.

We need to truly commit ourselves to those things we value and let go of unnecessary activities that have no or little value for us.

At the least, we can create more pockets of time in our everyday lives for the things we value most. Integrity is living true to our highest values.

Letting Go of Too Much Self-Centeredness (Kindness)

~~

*If you stop to be kind, you must
swerve often from your path.*

MARY WEBB

During my wife Julie's pregnancy with Jackson, our second child, she started having labor pains much too early. She took some medicine to help defer contractions but problems continued and our doctor finally determined that she would need to have twenty-four-hour bed rest. This was something very new for both of us and especially difficult for Julie.

At the beginning of each day I would put together an ice chest of food, and our two-and-a-half-year-old son, Adam, would stay in her bedroom with her during the day, doing a few simple tasks as well as a two-and-a-half-year-old could. This lasted for two months. At first I would come home from work and do the full course of chores (cooking, washing, shopping, errands, tending to Adam), still clinging to the idea of rushing through everything so that I would have time for what I wanted to do. My evening reading time was gone, as was my weekend hiking and other outdoor activities. I tried to be a helpful husband, but inside I was tense—I was used to time for "my stuff."

The stress of worrying about my stuff on top of everything else finally got to me and a bright light bulb went on in my head. I decided to simply surrender, stop rushing around, let go of self for a while, and simply focus on what I valued most: my wife and child (and child to be). I discovered that things really change when we let go of self. The whole experience was much less difficult, and I got everything done without the high frustration. Sometimes there would be a little residual time left over for the things I enjoyed, but if there wasn't, it didn't matter to me. I also developed much greater appreciation for all the many things Julie had been selflessly doing for us. This was a great life lesson, one that I conveniently forget all the time. There is something quite liberating when we surrender ourselves, let go of self, and simply do what needs to be done for others. As I found out, it can actually be liberating.

As with all of our instincts, our natural tendency to look out for "number one" has its advantages in the world of survival. By aggressively looking out for our own self-interests we ensure that we and our family will live to eat for another day. However, as with all of our survival instincts, if we feel and act on these impulses too often and for too long, they can be destructive. Looking out solely for number one can damage marriages, families, communities, and nations.

Selfishness is a natural, universal tendency for all of us. It doesn't matter if we're rich or poor, old or young, male or female, liberal or conservative, religious or nonreligious. If we completely look to our own self-interest without regard for others, it creates an unhealthy win–lose dynamic where we take what we want from others without consideration for their loss. That selfish behavior will untimately trample over everything we hold dear.

Kindness is a letting go of self. As with any other form of letting go, there is peace to be found in not clinging or grasping so much—in this case to ourselves. If we truly value others—especially those close to us—at least as much as we value ourselves, living true to those values requires that we look to their interests as much as to our own. Kindness requires that we practice letting go of our immediate needs and interests and focus for a time on the needs and interests of others. As Jürgen Habermas, the German sociologist and philosopher, emphasized, it begins by seeing people in everyday living as other selves, instead of seeing them simply as objects; as ends rather than as means.

Kindness is not only an action, it's an attitude. When we do the dishes, we can do them with ill grace or out of a desire to help our family. When we have conversations, we can focus on ourselves or focus on listening and supporting the other person. When there is only one piece of cake left, we can grab it or serve it to a loved one. When it would be easy to say something unkind or to pass along embarrassing gossip, we can let it go. Kindness is momentarily letting go of the strife and burden of self-interest. It is the peace of forgetting, at least for a moment, what we want others to do for us and living for the benefit of others without expecting anything at all in return. As Saint Therese of Lisieux once wrote, "When one loves, one does not calculate."

Some great souls in the world make kindness not only a part of their lives but the highest value in their lives. Agnes Gonxha Bojaxhiu grew up in Macedonia, the daughter of a construction contractor. She was quite close to her mother, Drana, a very religious and compassionate woman who instilled in her daughter a deep commitment to charity. Agnes eventually decided to become a nun, moved to Dublin, and took on the name of Sister Mary Teresa, named after Saint Therese of Lisieux. She moved to India, took her final vows, and became known as Mother Teresa.

For fifteen years Anges worked as a school teacher and principal, but living amid the extreme poverty in India, she felt that much more was needed and was "called" to serve the poorest of the poor. After six months of basic medical training, she went to Calcutta's poorest slums for the first time with no more specific goal than to aid "the unwanted, the unloved, the uncared for." Agnes began an open-air school for children and set up a home for the dying destitute. By the time of her death in 1997, her Missionaries of Charity numbered over 4,000—in addition to thousands of lay volunteers—with 610 foundations in 123 countries on all seven continents. Agnes's commitment to kindness became something much larger than her "self." She once wrote, "Every work of love is a work of peace, no matter how small it is."

The most fundamental form of kindness is living by the rule of no harm. But kindness can have many other faces: fairness, sympathy, compassion, mercy, patience, and providing a helping hand. Kindness is love in action. It's treating others as we would like to be treated on a proactive basis. Loving kindness is the binding, healing power within our human universe. It binds marriages, families, communities, and nations together. Hate and cruelty tear the world apart.

And the best time to let go of self and live a life of greater kindness is *right now*. As Henri-Frédéric Amiel wrote, "Life is short and we have not too much time for gladdening the hearts of those who are traveling the dark way with us. ... Make haste to be kind."

Forgiveness

Forgiveness is a special type of letting go of self. It is letting go of anger, resentment, and revenge when someone has done harm to us. When someone has harmed us, we have a natural human desire to want the other person to pay for that harm—to hurt as we hurt or to be punished for the injury they have caused. In a just society, there do indeed need to be consequences for harmful behavior, and for a time such feelings may feel justified. But there comes a time when there is no additional benefit to be found in continuing to hold on to angry and sorrowful emotions. As with all unpleasant emotions, we make our lives less peaceful when we enflame them further.

Community Service

Mother Teresa always maintained to her coworkers that the first acts of charity were most importantly experienced in the home: showing kindness to our spouses, children, and parents. Having a home of love and understanding is an important foundation for happiness. Community service expands this kindness to our neighborhood, city, and world.

In his book, *Wherever You Go, There You Are,* Jon Kabat-Zinn tells the story of Buckminster Fuller's brush with suicide at the age of thirty-two. Fuller had experienced a series of business failures, and in his depression he began to consider that his wife and young daughter would be better off without him. In the midst of this dark place, he developed a different solution: he decided to live from then on as though he *had* died. Being "dead" he wouldn't have to worry about how things worked out for him personally. The rest of his life would be a gift to the universe. His guiding question became, "What is it on this planet that needs doing that I know something about, that probably won't happen unless I take responsibility for it?" Kabat-Zinn phrases the question differently: "What is my job on the planet with a capital J?" or "What do I care about so much that I would pay to do it?"

Sharing ourselves with our communities is sharing our uniqueness in ways that leave the world a better place—in even the smallest ways. It's doing those things that may not get done in our communities unless we do them. Some people have the gift of music, art, scientific knowledge, political know-how, or athleticism. But others have the just-as-valuable gifts of listening, talking, sympathizing, peace-making, working hard, and getting important things done. We provide community service whenever we jump in, let go of self, and give of our own unique talents, traits, and ambitions. We are all humbled by those who have been willing to give up even life itself in order to provide service to their communities and countries. When we engage in community service, we take on the attitude of Lauren Myracle, evident in her declaration, "It's not what the universe gives us that matters, but what we give the universe."

Self-Kindness

Part of letting go of self means letting go of the burden of being too critical, harsh, and judgmental about self. We need to be at least as kind to ourselves as we are to other people. We need to think about ourselves and speak to ourselves as we would to a good friend. If we're forgiving of friends, we need to be forgiving of ourselves. In part this comes by fully accepting that we're simply human. We're regular, imperfect people living in an imperfect world. Until we fully accept ourselves on those terms, we will be bogged down by self. We will feel the pressure to overly protect ourselves and seek approval from others and may end up focusing too much energy and time on our emotional lives. We will likely be less selfish if we are first accepting and kind to ourselves. Being kind to ourselves frees us up emotionally to have more time and energy for others.

Whether it be in our own home, our city, or the world, we can do both inner and outer work to help us let go of the burden of too much self-centeredness in order to be kind to others:

- Practitioners of loving-kindness meditation suggest that we take time each day to be still and consciously invite words and feelings of kindness, compassion, and warm acceptance for the people in our lives. They suggest holding people in our mind's eye and wishing them all the best. When we wish blessings and peace upon people, it is more difficult to hold on to animosity. Such meditation typically begins with ourselves (self-kindness), basking in our own kindness and well-wishing, and then expands to loved ones, our community, humanity, and ultimately to those with whom we are not on good terms. Research on such meditation indicates that loving-kindness meditation has the added benefit of reducing stress levels.

- We can mentally remind ourselves of our love and compassion for our loved ones with the phrase, "I value you through thick and thin." When we truly value something, we cherish it and care for it. This should be at least as true for our important relationships as it would be for a new car or other prized material possessions.

- When there are chores to be done around the home, rather than assuming someone else will take care of them, we can let go of self and take care of them. We can practice more letting go of self by jumping into action on behalf of others.

- If there are important things that need to be done to help our friends, neighbors, or community, we can again practice letting go of self by jumping in and sharing our skills and energy. Our bodies were meant to do, and we can do much on behalf of others simply by jumping in and doing.

Kindness is basic to human experience. We all want to receive it, even when we don't give it. The Dalai Lama once wrote, "Our prime purpose in this life is to help others. And if we can't help them, at least don't hurt them."

SUMMARY FOR SKILL 15

Letting Go of Too Much
Self-Centeredness (Kindness)

Focusing too much on ourselves can be a stressful burden. It can get in the way of helping others and the world.

It can harm relationships with those we value most. Letting go of selfishness means surrendering our immediate interests and needs and seeing to the interests and needs of others.

We can practice this letting go of self-centeredness—or kindness—by jumping in and sharing our skills and energy on a daily basis, without making a big deal of it.

Such letting go can be both liberating and fulfilling.

SKILL 16

Letting Go of Frustration (Patience)

~~~

*We shall sooner have the fowl by hatching
the egg than by smashing it.*

ABRAHAM LINCOLN

By and large my father was an even-keeled man; and his five children are reasonably so. But he was also a naturally "antsy" person,
who was susceptible to episodes of frustration and impatience.
I've observed this in his children too. As we discovered in our
own parenting years, we had dormant volcanoes posing as regular
country hills quietly residing inside our heads. I didn't have the
energy that my father had in his fifties to chase down children
who smirked at him during a scolding, but I could certainly feel
and see various shades of red—well before my brain could think
a rational thought—if I was smirked at or fibbed to when I was
dealing with my own children. I completely know frustration. I
also know from first hand experience that "losing it" when we are
frustrated is not particularly productive.

In the tug and pull of life it's natural to feel frustration when
we can't easily and quickly get what we want. Frustration is not

all bad—it can prod us to action when it's needed. It can moti-vate us to take on important challenges. If something urgent or important needs to be dealt with—physical emergencies, eminent danger, or injustices—lack of frustration is no virtue. Mohandas Gandhi, Martin Luther King, and Cesar Chavez were driven in part by deep frustration with injustice and inhumanity. Nonethe-less, despite their frustrations, these three activists took on their lifelong causes with the highest form of patience—not giving up, not giving in, and not responding with rage.

Patience is learning to live with a certain amount of frustration without exploding and without giving up. In its simplest everyday form, patience is calm persistence. It's letting go of "hot" thoughts and emotions and moving toward more calm and resolute deter-mination, even in the midst of natural frustration. In the same way that courage is not the absence of fear but rather acting in the presence of fear, patience is not the absence of frustration but acting without anger and without giving up in the presence of frustration.

Whether it's the natural frustration of searching for a new job, dealing with boredom, learning a new skill, struggling with a misbehaving child, having to wait in lines or in traffic, or facing significant injustices, patience is nurtured by positive-thinking habits, acceptance, and action. Here are some examples:

- Changing unreasonable core beliefs that say that life should always be easy and fun
- Countering hot thoughts that might exaggerate how situations are, or the impulse to give up on something important because we feel frustrated
- Accepting our frustration as a natural emotional event
- Jumping in and doing whatever needs to be done, despite our natural frustrations or moods

Probably no public figure exemplified greater patience than Nelson Mandela. One of Mandela's most valuable accomplishments was achieving freedom for his fellow Africans in South Africa. Much of their land had been taken from them by colonists, and they were not allowed the basic freedoms of movement, speech, voting, or self-determination. They lived in a totalitarian state. Initially Mandela sought this freedom through nonviolent, political means, but when the government refused to provide basic rights to the larger African majority and enforced that refusal with violence, Mandela supported armed resistance. Because of this support he was put into prison for twenty-seven years from the ages forty-five to seventy-two. At one point he could have been released from prison if he had agreed to abandon his support for the efforts of freedom fighters, but he declined. He patiently lived with the degradations of a very difficult life in prison, spending much time working in a limestone quarry. When he was freed from prison, instead of indulging his anger, he let go of it and patiently worked toward building a unified nation. As Ralph Waldo Emerson wrote, "Patience and fortitude conquer all things."

Patience is especially important when it comes to those we love. If a low tolerance for frustration blinds us to understanding and accepting those we care about most, they will not feel our love. Unconditional love is unconditional. If we have developed habits of angry communication in response to frustration, we need to change our approach to communication, including apologizing when our emotions get the best of us. In general we need to place more value on our loved ones than our unpleasant emotions. As Paul of Tarsus wrote, "Love is patient." We don't have to love the imperfections of others, but if they're truly our loved ones, we do need to love *them*.

We practice patience by letting go of anger when we don't need it. To let go of it, we first need to see it. In our moments of feeling and seeing red, we need to allow our thinking to catch up with our feelings as best we can. We need to strive to calm down hot feelings with cooler thoughts. Scientists tell us that feelings are faster and often more powerful than thoughts, so it's pretty easy to be blinded by feelings. If it's difficult to immediately rein in strong frustration or anger, sometimes rather than attempting to think or talk our way through it, the best recourse is to separate ourselves for a cool-down period. It's a time to stop talking. Rather than saying or texting a single additional, potentially damaging word, we walk away and calm down. We go for a walk, listen to music, go to a movie, surf the web, or otherwise give ourselves a breather and a chance for our feelings to simmer down and allow us to relate to others on a calmer basis. Sometimes, letting go itself takes time and patience.

Patience is enhanced through cognitive- and acceptance-based strategies such as the following:

- We can occasionally remind ourselves of the larger truth that this imperfect life of ours has plenty of natural stress and frustration connected to it. Life is not naturally easy or without problems. Some amount of frustration is a normal part of human life.

- We can notice and modify exaggerated and inflexible thinking that makes things worse than they are. Instead of "This is terrible" thinking, we can respond with "It won't kill me" thinking. Instead of rehashing with "This is really, really crappy," we can remind ourselves that "I can deal with it." The content of our thoughts can make frustration worse than it needs to be. Applying reasonable optimism (nonnegative thinking) while in the midst of irritating and difficult situations can help reduce the intensity of frustration.

- The "bite" of everyday frustration is often not as strong as its "bark," once we pay attention to it. If we observe a sensation of frustration—whether prompted by bad traffic, difficult job tasks, hunger, or crying children—we quickly notice that the sensation itself is uncomfortable but not terrifying or physically incapacitating. If we so choose, we can simply accept the sensation of frustration for what it is—an unpleasantness—and persist in our pursuits.

- Beyond applying reasonable thinking and acceptance, we can each discover those outlets that help to calm us down in times of frustration. Taking breathers from frustration can enhance patience. This is not the same as giving up on what needs to be done but rather taking cool-down breaks by going for walks, sitting in a park, listening to music, or doing some other favorite personal activity that lessens frustration—or at least provides a temporary reprieve. This may not be Zen-like, but it is very practical.

- Behaviorists make the common-sense point that unhappiness is lessened if we engage in activities we enjoy or if we're in environments that make us feel good. If we can intersperse difficult tasks or situations that are frustrating for us with things we enjoy, all the better for our patience and staying power. For the past thirty years I have taken a daily walk at lunch out of pure enjoyment (I'm much like a dog that gets excited to go for its walk), and there is no doubt in my mind that behaviorists are correct in their advice to find pockets of time each day to do the things that bring us joy.

SUMMARY FOR SKILL 16

Letting Go of Frustration (Patience)

Frustration is a natural part of life. Patience isn't so much a lack of frustration and anger as it is not allowing frustration to prompt us to respond to life's difficult events with rage or by giving up.

We develop the skill of patience by pursuing the things that are important to us with persistent determination—again, not giving up or giving in but also not allowing anger to get in our way.

When we have particularly hot emotions, we let go of them as best we can, and we walk away and stop talking if we need to in order to preserve relationships that are important to us.

Letting Go of Fight and Flight (Assertiveness)

～～～

The best way out is always through.

ROBERT FROST

In our highly social human world, many of the threats we feel come from other people. While other people usually aren't literally threatening to physically harm us, they can be perceived as threats to our self-esteem, to our job, to what we want, or to other facets of our subjective well-being. Our emotions and bodies respond to these nonlethal threats as though they were physically threatening. Our automatic nervous system prepares our body for fight or flight. Fear and anger quickly kick into gear to energize our bodies. Cortisol flows into our blood stream, our heart rate surges, our muscles tighten, and we are prepared physically to deal with the threat. We are prepared to fight or to run away.

While fight or flight can work exceedingly well in certain life situations in which there is real danger involved, such responses can be counterproductive in many everyday social situations. Fighting over issues or avoiding social difficulties often doesn't solve problems and can ultimately harm ongoing human relationships. If we fight, problems can become worse and can tarnish personal relationships. If we flee or avoid, problems remain and persist and mean-spirited people can continue to manipulate or take advantage of us.

There is, however, a third response to difficult social situations: assertiveness. Assertiveness is not driven by our emotional/hormonal system (anger or fear) but by our mind. By consciously engaging in assertive social skills, we can let go of fight and flight responses (even if we still feel them) and engage in direct communication.

In 1955 Rosa Parks was a forty-two-year-old married seamstress in Montgomery, Alabama. She had been raised in the deeply segregated south, where white children rode buses to school, and black children were required to walk to theirs. As an adult she rode on buses in which black people were required to give up their seats for white people and take seats in the back. But Rosa was a quietly assertive person and on December 1, 1955, she refused to give up her bus seat for a white person. It is often thought that she did so because she was tired, but according to Rosa, this was not the case:

> "People always say that I didn't give up my seat because I was tired, but that isn't true. I was not tired physically, or no more tired than I usually was at the end of a working day. No, the only tired I was, was tired of giving in."

Rosa was arrested and sent to jail, but her act of assertiveness was a pivotal symbolic act in the American civil rights movement. Her arrest led to the successful boycott of buses and businesses by black citizens in Montgomery, which led to the greater prominence of a recently arrived minister in Montgomery, Martin Luther King. Rosa Parks did not physically fight or run, she simply and assertively let people know how she felt and what she wanted. In an interview in 1992 on National Public Radio, she said:

> "I did not want to be mistreated, I did not want to be deprived of a seat that I had paid for. It was just time . . . there was opportunity for me to take a stand to express the way I felt about being treated in that manner. I had not planned to get arrested. I had plenty to do without having to end up in jail. But when I had to face that decision, I didn't hesitate to do so because I felt that we had endured that too long. The more we gave in, the more we complied with that kind of treatment, the more oppressive it became."

Assertiveness does not mean aggression; it means clearly communicating our interests, feelings, and opinions using direct, honest, and firm communication without the intent of rolling over others. In difficult social interactions with people, we can let go of our natural fight-or-flight responses by instead using assertive social communication skills. When other people pose a threat to us by trying to fight us, take advantage of us, or ridicule or manipulate us, we can choose not to take the bait and respond with direct communication and action.

In his pioneering book on assertiveness, *When I Say No, I Feel Guilty*, Dr. Manuel Smith makes a list of personal rights of assertiveness. Among them are the simple rights to do the following:

- Choose our own behavior and thoughts without needing to bend to the manipulation of others
- Make mistakes and be responsible for them
- Offer no excuses or reasons if we choose not to
- Change our minds
- Be illogical

- Say "I don't know"
- Say "I don't understand"

We have the right to be responsible for our own lives and not allowing others to roll over us. First and foremost, assertiveness means letting go of our defensive mechanisms of fight or flight when encountering difficult social situations by engaging in open and direct communication that is firm when it needs to be.

In my book for young people, *Speak Up and Get Along!*, I compiled tools of assertiveness based on the work of specialists in the field of assertiveness training (including experts on dealing with school-yard teasing and bullying). The following sections include some of those basic tools.

Direct Assertive Communication

"I" STATEMENTS One of the most important elements of assertiveness is to simply disclose to people what we want and how we feel by using "I" statements. Directly expressing what we want and how we feel ensures that people clearly understand us. When people are being unkind, confrontational, manipulative, or critical, without getting defensive, we can simply use statements such as the following:

- "I don't like that . . ."
- "I disagree with . . ."
- "I want you to stop doing that . . ."
- "I feel irritated when you say that . . ."

Simple direct disclosure is also helpful when people ask us questions meant to be manipulative or ridiculing:

Question: "Why did you ...?"
Direct statement: "Because I wanted to."

Question: Why are you wearing ... ?
Direct statement: "Because I like it."

Question: How could you ...?
Direct statement: "Because I made a mistake."

If it's initially difficult emotionally for us to make direct statements, we can be honest about that as well when communicating with others, as long as we still state what we want or how we feel:

- "It's hard for me to say this, but I don't think that ..."
- "I hate to make a big deal, but I need to tell you that ..."
- "You may not like this, but I want you to ..."
- "Maybe nobody else has told you this, but I ..."

How we feel or what we think doesn't need to be logical or perfect. If we choose, we can have the freedom to say "I don't know," or "I don't understand" without the need for an excuse or qualification. Sometimes we need to help people understand how we want to be treated, and this is only possible by telling them so directly. We can be both direct and respectful. By asserting ourselves, we identify to others who we are and what we value. As Albert Camus wrote, "To know oneself, one should assert oneself."

SAYING NO Truly letting go includes letting go of doing things we don't want to do or of things we know aren't good for us. It's one thing to say yes to things we want to do, need to do, or feel right about. It's quite another to say yes out of habit, fear, or peer pressure. Our lives can become greatly defined by what we say yes or no to. Saying no, especially to friends and authority figures can sometimes be emotionally difficult. Because of this, finding comfortable ways to say no can be one of the most important social skills we will ever develop. Each of us needs to find our own comfortable phrasing for saying no in situations that are hard for us. There are many ways to get there:

- "No, but thanks for asking."
- "No, I won't be able to."
- "I'm sorry, but I can't"
- "It's hard for me to say this, but no."
- "You might not like this, but I just can't."
- "Sounds fun, but I'm going to have to pass."
- "No, no, a thousand times no!"

It's not how we say no but that we do eventually say it when we need to.

ASKING SIMPLE QUESTIONS With "I" statements we *say* what we want or need, and with simple questions we *ask* for what we want or need. As regular human beings we need to accept the reality that we're not perfect. We don't know all things, we don't understand all things, we don't always pay attention, we get bored, and we get lost (though we males are loathe to ever admit it). Sometimes people who are deemed less educated know a lot more than we do. We liberate ourselves when we learn to humble ourselves to ask any question at any time. We are imprisoned to the extent that pride and peer pressure (not wanting to look dumb or imperfect around others) keep us from asking questions. Individuals, families, companies, and nations waste great amounts of time, energy, money, and even lives by not asking "Why?" or "Why not?" Only when we get clear answers to simple questions can we make reasonable choices. Richard Feynman, one of the world's leading physicists, maintained that we should always be suspicious of ideas that can't be simply explained. For Feynman, the important simple question (especially when it comes to being told things by "experts") was "How did they find that out?" There are many ways to ask simple questions even if we feel uncomfortable emotionally doing it:

- "I'm still not getting it; could you explain it again?"
- "This may sound dumb, but why?"
- "Could you please go over that again?"
- "For some reason I'm still not getting it. Could you explain it one more time?"

Or more directly:

- "Why?" "Why not?" "What if?"
- "Why that way?" "How do they know that?" "What does that mean?"
- "Why does this matter?"

If it's embarrassing for us to ask questions in certain situations, it's time to ask ourselves another question, "What's the worst that could happen by asking this question?"

The simple questions of "Why?" or "Why not?" or "Why would that be true?" also can be used effectively to fend off the bossy, demeaning statements of others, such as: "You really shouldn't do that" or "You should know better."

OFFERING SOLUTIONS Conflict is at the hub of most difficult human interaction. A certain amount of conflict in human relations is normal and to be expected. People have their own needs, interests, and opinions and sometimes they need to stand up strongly for them. Mean-spirited people with harmful intent need to be confronted and opposed. But there is much everyday conflict that can be quite unnecessary, including confrontations at home, work, and in the nitty-gritty world of the marketplace. We don't need to simply roll over and give in in order to resolve conflict, but we can apply assertive leadership by initiating and offering solutions (as described in the chapter on pages 73–75, on solution thinking).

We can lead first with a direct expression of how we feel and what we want but simultaneously have the attitude that "we need to come up with a reasonable solution that's fair for both of us." In our most important personal relationships, it is especially critical to break out of patterns of emotionally driven conflict, use reasonable thinking to place value on the other person, and return to a mode of solution-mindedness. On the other hand, if a person is simply acting as a manipulative bully, we must either try to find a neutral form of mediation (a referee) or walk away.

Dealing with Blame and Manipulation

MEA CULPA It's not naturally easy in human interaction to deal with criticism. Sometimes criticism is valid and helpful, but for many of us, it's not always easy to accept emotionally. Blame can feel like a threat. The most assertive communication tool we can use when it comes to valid blame is to honestly own up to it rather than attempting to fight over it or avoid it. *Mea culpa* means "my fault" in Latin, and it communicates the following:

- "You're right, that was a mistake; I'll make up for it."
- "Yes, that was my fault; I should have done it differently."
- "You're correct—that was not a good idea."

It's as natural as the sun rising for us humans to make mistakes; and it's just as natural for us (males, in particular) not to want to admit to them. When we use a mea culpa, we are choosing not to argue, get defensive, or make excuses. We are choosing to simply agree with the person who is blaming us and apologize for what we've done. But a mea culpa doesn't just mean using direct expression, it means really taking responsibility for a mistake and making up for it as best we can.

On the other hand, if blame is misplaced, it's a mistake to let it go unchallenged. It's just as important to clear up any blame that we don't deserve as it is to take responsibility when we do deserve it. If we don't set the record straight, people may simply assume that silence is an indication of guilt. We may develop a reputation that does us no good because of false information. People still may not believe us, but it can be quite important to assertively set the record straight with respect to false blame and false rumors.

"MAYBE" PHRASING Sometimes blame is an emotional outburst meant to communicate anger and hurt and to punish. And sometimes blame or ridicule is meant to demean or bully. Along with simply and clearly expressing how we feel when people talk to us that way (expressing what we don't like), conditional "maybe" phrasing can be used in situations in which blame or judgmental comments are meant to belittle us. Possibilities include the following:

- "That might be true."
- "You might be right."
- "Maybe."
- "Could be."
- "Possibly."

"Maybe" phrasing can be especially helpful in answering questions that are meant to demean. It leaves others with little else to say and thus does not reward manipulation.

Question: "Aren't you acting a little too . . .?"
Maybe phrase: "Maybe, but that's just how I am."

Question: "Isn't it weird that you . . .?"
Maybe phrase: "You could be right."

"YOU" STATEMENTS Sometimes people try to manipulate and roll over others for no other reason than because they are domineering, because they can, or because they're mean-spirited. Sometimes, conditional "maybe" phrasing doesn't feel empowering enough in such situations, and we really want these people to stop. In addition to directly expressing how we feel and what we want with "I" statements, we can also use "you" statements to point out why they're wrong and to direct the attention and onus back on them.

Other: "You have a very irritating laugh."
You: "Maybe so. But I don't like you speaking to me in that way."

Other: "You've come into this meeting completely unprepared. What's your problem?"
You: "I did prepare for the meeting, though apparently not to your liking. I would appreciate it, however, if you would just tell me what you want rather than speaking to me like that."

Other: "I can't believe that you would act like such an idiot."
You: "And I can't believe that you would actually talk to anyone that way."

We need to teach some people how we want to be treated, and beyond direct "I" statements, sometimes "you" statements can help get us there.

PERSISTENCE Without persistence, assertive communication skills may not be effective. If I express my reasonable wants and feelings and they are not heard, I need to express them until I get a reasonable response. If I work for an organization and have a complaint, I need to go up the chain of command until I reach someone who can do something about my reasonable concerns. If I say no, and others continue to press me to say yes, I need to ultimately succeed with my no, if it's something I really don't want to do. If others are trying to manipulate me to get their way or to make me feel inferior, I need to respond until they stop or until I decide I don't want be in conversation with them. If I'm seeking to resolve a conflict with a loved one, I need to keep offering solutions until one works. One of the key elements of effective assertiveness is to be a "squeaky wheel." Unless, of course, a real physical threat is in play, in which case our fight-or-flight emotions are sending the right signal!

The Boogeyman

In our interactions with others, it is helpful to gradually get desensitized to the opinion and pressure of others. We need to develop a thicker skin. Socrates referred to the opinion of others as the "boogeyman." This boogeyman can keep us from doing the right thing and can pressure us to do the wrong thing. It can keep us from living the full measure of who we are and what we want to do. Living happily and honestly ultimately requires learning to be more comfortable with disapproval. It means letting go of the opinions of others as a constricting force in our lives. Socrates suggested that we strive to overcome our fear of the boogeyman, of peer pressure, and ridicule, just as children eventually overcome their fear of monsters in the dark.

Besides developing and using assertive communication skills, it can also help to learn to accept the reality that there are difficult people in the world. It may not feel good, we may not like it, but if we accept rather than struggle over this fact, we can still function in the face of it. Unless we face a physical threat, we have no need to avoid mean people and can accept the unpleasantness of being in their presence, just as we can learn to accept experiencing any unpleasant sensation. In the case of unpleasant people, we accept the emotions we feel in their presence and continue to do whatever we need to in their presence, despite these emotions.

This in no way means that we should seek out the acceptance or friendship of people who are consistently mean to us or others. As a youth advocate with some understanding of the issue of bullying in schools, I have found that according to experts, a uniquely difficult phenomenon with bullies and victims is that sometimes victims so much want to be accepted by their tormentors that they continue to hang out with the very people who are abusive to them. They'd rather have the acceptance and friendship of bullies than realize that mean people aren't good for them. There is evidence that this happens with adults as well. Accepting that there are mean, irritating people and being able to interact independently in their presence is one thing; needing or seeking out the acceptance and friendship of such people is quite another. There is never a good reason to seek out or remain in a relationship with a person who is consistently mean or abusive to us.

SUMMARY FOR SKILL 17

Letting Go of Fight and Flight (Assertiveness)

A natural, biological response to perceived threats in life is to fight or run away. This works well when we have physical threats, but not very well at all in dealing with people problems that are not physically threatening.

Fighting can harm relationships, and avoidance leaves problems unresolved.

Assertiveness is letting go of fight and flight by developing the skill of directly expressing how we feel and what we want without rolling over others.

Various modes of assertiveness include: direct expression using "I" statements, learning to comfortably say no, asking simple questions, assertively offering solutions to conflict, directly accepting blame when it's deserved, using conditional "maybe" and "you" statements to deal with manipulation, and being persistent as needed.

Meditation for the Nonpractitioner

∿

There are many varieties of meditation, but
what they generally have in common are techniques
for making the mind peaceful.

THE DALAI LAMA

I have great respect for the Buddhist commitment to the benefits of formal mindfulness meditation. However, I must admit that some of my most peaceful, enjoyable moments have been the result of mindlessness, absentmindedness, daydreaming, and unintentional wandering. Sometimes when I'm in a zone (a "flow" as it's sometimes called), I'm not at all mindful of any zone. I'm blissfully ignoring everything else around me (to family members' and coworkers' chagrin). For me, this sometimes happens when adventuring in the outdoors, playing a sport, reading, gardening, doing certain work projects, or simply thinking about an issue or question that is interesting or important to me.

Mindfulness experts might say that I'm mindfully focused, but it honestly feels like I'm not mindful at all. It feels like I'm completely hypoconsciously lost in the moment. But as Siddhartha

Gautama (the original Buddha) taught, if we get too technical or definitional about these things, we're probably missing the point. When he was near death, he reportedly told his disciples to "be your own lamps." In other words, figure out what works for you and don't get too caught up in terminology and orthodox technique. What works for others (including gurus) may have no relevance for your life. One of the key points of any form of meditation practice is to make the mind peaceful, so that the monkey jumping around in our heads doesn't stop us from living our lives. But how we get there, is up to us.

The vast majority of us don't have a routine of formal meditation practice or any intention of starting one, but most of us do have an innate interest in "making the mind peaceful"—we want to feel good inside at least part of the time. Even if by nature we have a more easygoing temperament, we all are still faced with (1) imperfect, unpleasant thoughts and emotions, (2) difficult life events, and (3) some measure of natural pain and suffering, either physically or emotionally. If we struggle with feelings of unhappiness, it's only natural that we try to feel better through the most obvious external means: participating in activities we enjoy, avoiding things we don't enjoy, and maybe reaching out for the companionship and comfort of friends, family, or trusted counselors. If we have real difficulty in making the mind peaceful, we may turn to professional medical help.

The advantage of discovering for ourselves a more formal, *internal* practice to help in making the mind peaceful is that internal practices are portable and can be turned to in the midst of everyday living. Over time they may help us to become more naturally peaceful inside. Trying to feel good solely by externally chasing after comfort and avoiding discomfort can keep us from engaging fully in our everyday lives; it can prevent us from living true to our values and pursuing our aspirations. In the end such chasing/avoiding doesn't guarantee that we won't end up right back in the same spot.

We need approaches that help us to have less internal turmoil in the midst of life, not in the avoidance of life. Solely using external approaches to making the mind peaceful is simply not enough. We will still experience our own natural emotions, which do not simply disappear. There have been plenty of depressed people who have been very effective in external pursuits (star athletes, talented artists, popular Hollywood personalities, successful billionaires) and plenty of chronically unhappy people who have had supportive family, friends, and counselors. Working on internal well-being solely from the outside-in clearly is not sufficient. Our well-being requires internal work and practice as well.

When I was young, one of my great passions was playing basketball. I spent hour upon hour shooting baskets by myself. I sought out pickup games wherever I could find them, any time of the year—rain or shine. I became a reasonably good player in a small-town environment, and it taught me the obvious benefits of practice. It's no big secret that we become more and more proficient at the things we practice, as my wife will also confirm from her many years of teaching piano to young people. So too it is with making the mind peaceful. Some of us may be born with the type of temperament or inherent skill to be reasonably peaceful inside—not unlike naturally talented athletes or musicians. But it's just as likely that most of us can benefit by developing this skill further and enhancing it by practice. Meditation can be looked upon as a practice to make the mind peaceful, so that we get better at applying this skill in everyday living.

In the same way that reasonable optimism isn't so much positive thinking but rather nonnegative thinking, making the mind peaceful may not be so much peaceful thinking (though this can provide a pleasant reprieve from daily stress) as it is calmly accepting our natural, imperfect emotions. Rather than thinking about peace, we learn to accept nonpeaceful thoughts and emotions with greater calmness. Rather than trying to shove out pain and suffering (which can be counterproductive), we observe and accept them as part of life. Whatever approach we use, we need it to be something that we can use in everyday living. If we want to have greater peace of mind in the midst of the daily imperfections and struggles of life, we need an approach that helps us to accept and be open to life rather than prompting us to avoid and close off the life we were meant to experience.

Trying any form of meditation to practice making the mind peaceful requires practicing a particular mindset. It requires the following:

- More actively engaging our transcendent "observing self"—the independent, perspective-taking part of us that observes everything else, including our thoughts and feelings
- Simply observing thoughts and feelings rather than overidentifying with or becoming those thoughts and feelings
- Letting go of judgment and criticism and being completely open and accepting of mental events—including unpleasant thoughts and emotions—rather than avoiding or fighting them

Meditation practice, for practitioners and nonpractitioners alike, is practicing using our "observing self" to simply be and to nonjudgmentally and calmly monitor our internal and external worlds.

All of the following forms of meditation can be practiced quite formally, but each of us can develop our own less formal, nonpractitioner tools and approaches to help us settle the mud in the thought- and emotion-producing stream that is our mind.

Mindfulness

Mindfulness is generally defined simply as paying attention in the present moment, on purpose and without judgment. A very basic approach to mindfulness meditation is to sit quietly and pay attention to one's breathing, letting go of all the other activities of the mind, returning to a gentle focus on the breathing when the mind drifts away. This same mindful attention can be applied to most any other object or activity: listening, walking, eating, driving, cooking, etc. In some forms of very concentrative meditation (e.g., Transcendental Meditation), the focus is on a single word, or mantra. In forms of very open awareness meditation (e.g., Zazen), practitioners open the mind into a panoramic awareness of whatever is happening without a specific focus—the key remains paying attention in the present moment without judging whatever is happening.

Guided Visualization

Guided visualization is visually focusing on objects with the mind's eye; again, calmly paying attention without judgment. For example sometimes this is done by doing a "body scan": slowly visualizing each part of the body while simultaneously relaxing that part of the body. An even more simple, nonpractitioner approach is to visualize our favorite places or people and keep them in our hearts, basking in the peacefulness of the moment (one of my personal favorite visualizations is sitting by a brook in the forest). Guided visualization can also be used to work with the parts of life that bring us unhappiness—focusing on a fear or pain through visualization and applying nonjudgmental acceptance can be undertaken in order to become less sensitized to that fear or pain.

Loving-Kindness Meditation

This is a form of mindfulness meditation and visualization for which we sit calmly and visualize or think about other people with kindness and compassion. We turn our attention to family members, friends, neighbors, and even those with whom we don't have a good relationship and wish them the best. We do the same for ourselves. This has the advantage of not only making our minds more peaceful but helping us develop attitudes of greater kindness toward others.

Yoga

In its mindfulness form, yoga isn't just a relaxing physical exercise, it's another form of meditation. Instead of using the breath or a mantra as the point of mindful focus, the body and yoga positions become the focus of mindfulness. One nonjudgmentally pays attention in the present moment to the body as movements and positions are taken. The same is true of tai chi (making soft martial arts movements) and any other intentional physical exercise or activity.

Contemplation

For the nonpractitioner, focusing on any topic of value to us and reviewing it with openness can be very helpful to our lives in general. Sometimes we get so caught up in automatic everyday living that we don't take time to fully and consciously consider and examine. In a calmer frame of mind, contemplation can mean taking the time to examine our beliefs to make sure they are reasonable and work well for us (have positive cash value); to consider and determine what we value most (our core values) and the commitments we are willing to make to those values; to consider new actions and directions we might want to take in our lives; or to simply think on and reconfirm with gratitude the blessings of our lives. Contemplation means giving ourselves some breathing room just to more calmly and wisely observe and consider issues that are important to us, and to jot down useful or inspiring ideas that come out of that process.

Prayer

For people of faith, prayer is resting in God or in the Universe. It is taking the time to unload one's burdens, seek out strength of spirit, and express gratitude. The tradition of centering prayer is similar to more formal meditation in that the practitioner focuses on a sacred word ("God," "Lord," "love," "peace") and gently returns to that word if the mind drifts away. Some forms of more formal prayer (Lectio Divina) are carried out by reading a verse of sacred scripture and observing insights. Mother Teresa once wrote, "We need to be alone with God in silence to be renewed and transformed. Silence gives a new outlook on life. In it we are filled with the grace of God. ..." For some people, simply being in nature—sitting by a stream or walking through a park—can provide a sense of awe or a connection to the sacred that contributes to making the mind peaceful.

Flow Activities

When we participate in flow activities, our minds are not in turmoil or struggle, they are absorbed by the activity itself. Depending on who we are, working on computers, watching a movie, playing a musical instrument, painting, cycling, reading, swimming, etc., can all be flow activities. Behaviorists keep reminding us that the more we do of what we really enjoy, the better our well-being.

Rest

Rest of course is one of the most natural and effective avenues for nonpractitioners to make the mind peaceful. The Dalai Lama once observed that "sleep is the best form of meditation." Ancient Israel set aside an entire day, the Sabbath, for the very purpose of resting from everyday work and worries. Even if we find it hard to set aside full days for rest, finding restful moments throughout our days can pay dividends to our well-being. Of course, to be truly restful, physical rest must translate into mental rest. If it doesn't,

then some of the more conscious approaches to meditation men-
tioned above become all the more helpful. In some form, to truly
rest, we still need to let go of mental turmoil and worry; and this
is usually best accomplished by practicing greater nonjudgmental
acceptance.

Radical Acceptance

Radical acceptance is taking a breather from everyday analysis
and judgment and literally accepting all of life as it is in the present moment. Accepting does not mean agreeing with everything
or liking it. It doesn't mean not changing whatever needs to be
changed. It's simply seeing life for what it is in this moment. It's
accepting reality, without the turmoil. It can be very tiring to fight
reality. Not accepting the painful, unpleasant side of life can simply
lead to greater suffering. Instead of saying, "I hate this situation,"
we can try, "I'm in this situation. I don't like it, and if I can change
it I will, but it is part of life." "It is what it is" need not be an attitude of resignation but an attitude of not adding to the turmoil
of life's difficulties. Radical acceptance is a ready-at-hand tool for
the nonpractitioner on a daily basis. Even brief moments of radical
acceptance, or ending the day by sitting back and simply letting
the universe be, or letting God take care of the universe, can be
refreshing.

SUMMARY FOR SKILL 18

Meditation for the Nonpractitioner

Most of us have an innate interest in making the mind peaceful in the midst of our everyday living.

We want to feel good inside at least part of the time, and simply chasing after pleasure and avoiding pain won't do.

We still experience our natural emotions, which don't just disappear. Thus, to some extent, making the mind peaceful requires inner attention and work.

We don't need to be a formal meditation practitioner to practice making the mind peaceful, but we can experiment and discover the tools that work best for us.

Some of the tools described in this chapter include mindfulness, guided visualization, loving-kindness meditation, yoga, contemplation, prayer, flow activities, rest, and radical acceptance. These can be approached on both an informal and a formal basis.

The Nonpursuit of Happiness

The pursuit of happiness is often thought of in external terms: family, friends, career, material goods, health, fun, personal interests, and causes. But as we all know, people can successfully experience many of those external elements of happiness and still not be happy inside. At the end of the day, subjective well-being is *internal*, and much of this internal well-being results not from an effort to obtain but from the intentional activity of letting go.

The clear reality is that we simply do not live in a continuously happy world. We do not always have happy thoughts and feelings. Things don't always go well, and in fact sometimes they go terribly badly. Even if the external world smiles upon us, peace and happiness are only two of the many emotions we are meant to naturally feel. The obvious truth is that we are naturally meant to experience sadness, suffering, grief, fear, anger, guilt, and pain. Some level of psychological suffering is a basic characteristic of human life. Because of this human condition, it's to be expected that we don't experience ongoing bliss, and we don't need to. We just need to be able to live our lives in the midst of these imperfect emotions.

To become overly attached to the goal of happiness can ironically reduce the quality of our inner lives. Our well-being is not enhanced so much by chasing after happiness (in the form of more pleasure, wealth, and ease) but in letting go of the sources of unhappiness. Most fundamentally we can begin to practice and develop the following skills:

- Noticing and modifying overly negative, inflexible harsh thinking
- Reviewing and gradually upgrading unreasonable beliefs and labels about ourselves, others, and the world that contain little or no cash value toward well-being
- Changing harmful behavior by creating solutions, making new commitments, and jumping into new behaviors
- Letting go of the turmoil related to holding on to unpleasant events, thoughts, or emotions that aren't important or that we cannot easily change, by practicing nonjudgmental awareness and acceptance

We human beings are indeed meant to be on this planet, and like Odysseus in the *Odyssey*, we are also meant to experience a challenging journey while here—however short or long. We are not only faced with the challenges of living in a physically imperfect world (filled with scarcity, sickness, and dangers as well as monotony), but we are also faced with the challenges of living with our own imperfect mental and emotional worlds (temperaments, moods, and distorted beliefs and perceptions). So no matter how perfect one part of our life may be, there is another challenge just around the bend to make sure our lives are not problem-free! As long as we live in an imperfect, hazardous world and have the ability to understand, experience, and feel both the good and the bad (unlike many of our fellow living creatures), we are compelled to live a life with problems and struggles.

Our advanced mind and deep emotions open us up to an understanding and a full experience of the difficulties of life, but they also provide us with gateways to well-being. Our minds are more than the events, thoughts, and emotions that simply come to us. We have the ability to choose our highest values and to chart (and rechart) our course. We have the ability to make commitments and to jump in even when we're afraid, to mindfully pay attention to life's moments with less judgment, and to more peacefully accept physical and emotional difficulty. We have the opportunity to more fully love family and friends, to experience and develop our unique skills and talents, to experience nature, beauty, and the sacred, to endure, transform, and overcome.

Ultimately, we are gifted with the ability to enhance our personal well-being through the power of thought and through the peace of letting go.

SELECTED BIBLIOGRAPHY

Adams, James. *The Care and Feeding of Ideas: A Guide to Encouraging Creativity.* Boston: Da Capo Press, 1986.

Beck, Judith S. *Cognitive Behavior Therapy: The Basics and Beyond* (2nd edition). New York: The Guilford Press, 2011.

Burns, David D. *Feeling Good: The New Mood Therapy.* New York: William Morrow, 1980.

Butler, A.C.; J.E. Chapman; E.M. Forman; and A.T. Beck. (2006). "The Empirical Status of Cognitive-Behavioral Therapy: A Review of Meta-Analyses," *Clinical Psychology Review* 26 (1): 17–31.

Cohen, S. Marc, Patricia Curd and C.D.C. Reeve, eds. *Readings in Ancient Greek Philosophy.* Indianapolis: Hackett Publishing, 2005.

Cummings, E.E. *100 Selected Poems.* New York: Grove Press, 1994.

The Dalai Lama and Howard Cutler. *The Art of Happiness: A Handbook for Living.* New York: Riverhead Books, 1998.

Davis, D.M., and J.A Hayes. (2011). "What Are the Benefits of Mindfulness? A Practice Review of Psychotherapy-Related Research," *Psychotherapy*, 48 (2): 198–208.

Denton, Michael. *Nature's Destiny: How the Laws of Biology Reveal Purpose in the Universe.* New York: The Free Press, 1998.

Diener, Ed, and Robert Biswas-Diener. *Happiness: Unlocking the Mysteries of Psychological Wealth*. Malden, MA: Blackwell Publishing, 2008.

Feng, Gia-Fu, and Jane English, trans. *Tao Te Ching*. New York: Vintage Books, 1972.

Frankl, Victor. *Man's Search for Meaning*. Boston: Beacon Press, 2006 (originally published in 1946).

Gethin, Rupert. *Sayings of the Buddha: New Translations from the Pali Nikaya* (Oxford World's Classics). Oxford: Oxford University Press, 2008.

Goleman, Daniel. *Emotional Intelligence*. New York: Bantam Books, 1995.

Hanh, Thich Nhat. *Peace Is Every Step*. New York: Bantam Books, 1990.

Hammond, John; Ralph Keeney, and Howard Raiffa. *Smart Choices: A Practical Guide to Making Better Decisions*. New York: Crown Business, 2002.

Hayes, J.A., A. Masuda, R. Bissett, J. Luoma, and L.F. Guerrero. (2004). "DBT, FAP, and ACT: How Empirically Oriented Are the New Therapy Technologies?" *Behavior Therapy*, 35–54.

Hayes, Steven C., Victoria M. Follette, and Marsha M. Linehan. *Mindfulness and Acceptance*. New York: The Guilford Press, 2004.

Hayes, Steven C., Kirk D. Strosahl, and Kelly G. Wilson. *Acceptance and Commitment Therapy: The Process and Practice of Mindful Change* (2nd edition) New York: The Guilford Press, 2012.

Hick, John. *The New Frontier of Religion and Science*. New York: Palgrave MacMillan, 2010.

Hood, R.W., B. Spilka, B. Hunsberger, and R.L. Gorsuch, *The Psychology of Religion: An Empirical Approach*. New York: The Guilford Press, 1996.

James, William. *Pragmatism.* Indianapolis: Hackett Publishing Company, 1981 (originally published in 1907).

——. *The Varieties of Religious Experience.* New York: Random House/ Modern Library Edition, 1994 (originally published in 1902).

Kabat-Zinn, Jon. *Full Catastrophe Living.* New York: Delta, 1990.

——. *Wherever You Go There You Are.* New York: Hyperion, 1994.

Lanza, Robert. *Biocentrism: How Life and Consciousness Are the Keys to Understanding the True Nature of the Universe.* Dallas: BanBella Books, 2009.

Lewis, C.S. *A Grief Observed.* New York: Harper One, 1961.

McGinn, Colin. *The Mysterious Flame: Conscious Minds in a Material World.* New York: Basic Books, 1999.

Nadler, Gerald, and Shozo Hibino. *Breakthrough Thinking: Seven Principles of Creative Problem Solving.* Roseville, CA: Prima Lifestyles, 1994.

Parks, Rosa, and James Haskins. *Rosa Parks: My Story.* New York: Dial Books, 1992.

Rosenblum, Bruce, and Fred Kuttner. *Quantum Enigma: Physics Encounters Consciousness.* Oxford: Oxford University Press, 2006.

Schafer, Lothar. *Infinite Potential: What Quantum Physics Reveals about How We Should Live.* New York: Deepak Chopra Books, 2011.

Seligman, Martin. *Learned Optimism: How to Change Your Mind and Your Life.* New York: Pocket Books, 1990.

Smith, Manuel J. *When I Say No, I Feel Guilty.* New York: Bantam Books, 1975.

Wallace, B. Alan. *The Taboo of Subjectivity: Toward a New Science of Consciousness.* Oxford: Oxford University Press, 2000.

AUTHOR BIOGRAPHY

SCOTT COOPER is a national youth advocate and writer, with a special focus on coping skills for young people. His previous books include the award-winning *Speak Up and Get Along* (Free Spirit Press) and *Sticks and Stones* (Random House/Crown). His new book, *Rock and Water*, provides practical, research-based tools to help enhance the well-being of adults, and is based on modern cognitive- and acceptance-based approaches to everyday living. Cooper lives in Northern California, where he is also a COO in private industry.